lonely planet

D0206315

ICELAND'S RING ROAD

ROAD TRIPS

This edition written and researched by

Andy Symington, Alexis Averbuck, Carolyn Bain

HOW TO USE THIS BOOK

Reviews

In the Destinations section:

All reviews are ordered in our authors' preference, starting with their most preferred option. Additionally:

Sights are arranged in the geographic order that we suggest you visit them and, within this order, by author preference.

Eating and Sleeping reviews are ordered by price range (budget, midrange, top end) and, within these ranges, by author preference.

Map Legend

Routes

▬▬ Trip Route
▬▬ Trip Detour
░░░ Linked Trip
▬▶ Walk Route
▭▭ Tollway
▭▭ Freeway
▭▭ Primary
▭▭ Secondary
▭▭ Tertiary
▭▭ Lane
▭▭ Unsealed Road
◇◇◇ Plaza/Mall
∷∷∷ Steps
)=(Tunnel
▭▭▭ Pedestrian
       Overpass
--- Walk Track/Path

Boundaries

--- International
----- State/Province
━━ Cliff

Hydrography

〜 River/Creek
〜 Intermittent River
〜 Swamp/Mangrove
〜 Canal
▭ Water
▭ Dry/Salt/
    Intermittent Lake
▭ Glacier

Highway Markers

[A20] Highway marker

Trips

[1] Trip Numbers
[9] Trip Stop
[🏃] Walking tour
[↪] Trip Detour

Population

◉ Capital (National)
◉ Capital
    (State/Province)
● City/Large Town
● Town/Village

Areas

▒ Beach
▒ Glacier
+++ Cemetery
       (Christian)
××× Cemetery (Other)
▒ Park
▒ Forest
▒ Reservation
▒ Urban Area
▒ Sportsground

Transport

✈ Airport
↦Ⓑ↤ Cable Car/
       Funicular
Ⓜ Metro station
Ⓟ Parking
↦Ⓡ↤ Train/Railway
↦Ⓣ↤ Tram

Note: Not all symbols displayed above appear on the maps in this book

Symbols In This Book

✓	Top Tips	🍷	Food & Drink
🔗	Link Your Trips	🌳	Outdoors
💬	Tips from Locals	📷	Essential Photo
↪	Trip Detour	🏃	Walking Tour
📖	History & Culture	🍴	Eating
👫	Family	🛏	Sleeping

◉	Sights	🛏	Sleeping
🏖	Beaches	🍴	Eating
🏃	Activities	🍷	Drinking
🎓	Courses	☆	Entertainment
👉	Tours	🛍	Shopping
✳	Festivals & Events	ⓘ	Information & Transport

These symbols and abbreviations give vital information for each listing:

📞	Telephone number	🐾	Pet-friendly
⊙	Opening hours	🚌	Bus
P	Parking	⛴	Ferry
⊖	Nonsmoking	🚊	Tram
❄	Air-conditioning	🚆	Train
@	Internet access	apt	apartments
🛜	Wi-fi access	d	double rooms
🏊	Swimming pool	dm	dorm beds
🥗	Vegetarian selection	q	quad rooms
📋	English-language menu	r	rooms
👪	Family-friendly	s	single rooms
		ste	suites
		tr	triple rooms
		tw	twin rooms

CONTENTS

PLAN YOUR TRIP

ROAD TRIPS

DESTINATIONS

ROAD TRIP ESSENTIALS.... 118

Eldhraun (p36)

WELCOME TO
ICELAND'S RING ROAD

Hitting headlines, topping bucket lists, wooing nature lovers and dazzling increasing numbers of visitors: Iceland, an underpopulated island marooned near the top of the globe, is literally a country in the making. It's a vast volcanic laboratory where mighty forces shape the earth: geysers gush, mudpots gloop, ice-covered volcanoes rumble and glaciers cut great pathways through the mountains. Its supercharged splendour seems designed to remind visitors of their utter insignificance in the greater scheme of things.

Bravely forging through the geological magnificence is the Ring Road, Iceland's Route 1, which joins nearly all the places you can get to without a serious 4WD in one long circumnavigation of the island. Epic doesn't even begin to describe this road trip, but it's not only about jaw-dropping vistas: the counterpoint to so much natural beauty is found in Iceland's vibrant cultural life, handicrafts, locavore cuisine and the warmth of its creative, no-nonsense, welcoming people. It's a drive like no other.

→

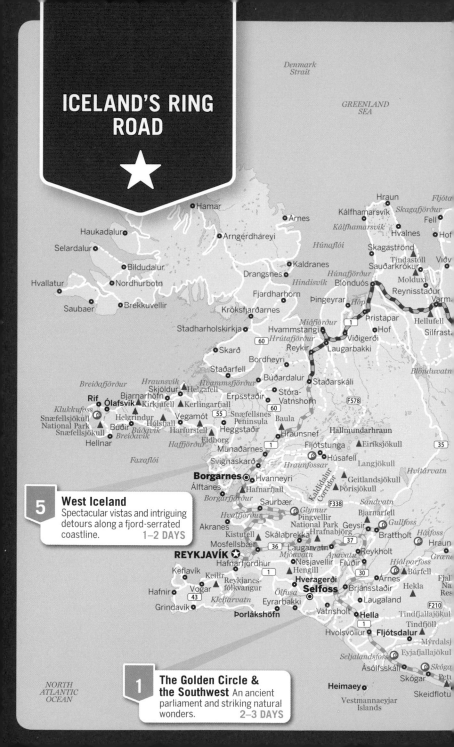

ICELAND'S RING ROAD

★

Denmark Strait

GREENLAND SEA

Hamar

Haukadalur

Selardalur

Bildudalur

Hvallatur   Nordhurbotn

Saubaer   Brekkuvellir

Árnes

Hraun

Kálfhamarsvík   Skagafjörður   Fljóta

Kálfhamarsvík   Fell

Hvalnes   Hof

Arngerdháreyi

Húnaflói   Skagaströnd

Tindastóll   Viðv

Kaldranes   Sauðárkrókur

Drangsnes   Húnafjörður   Molduxi

Hindisvík   Blönduós   Reynisstaðir

Fjardharhorn   Þingeyrar   Hóp   Varma

Króksfjarðarnes   Þristapar   Hellufell

Miðfjörður   Hof   Silfrast

Stadharholkirkja   Hvammstangi   Viðigerði

Hrútafjörður   Reykir   Laugarbakki

Skarð   Bordheyri   Blönduvatn

Staðarfell   Búðardalur   Staðarskáli

Breiðafjörður   Hraunsvík   Hvammsfjörður

Skjöldur   Helgafell   Erpsstaðir   Stóra-

Rif   Bjarnarhöfn   Vatnshorn

Klukkufoss   Ólafsvík   Kirkjufell   Kerlingarfjall   F578

Snæfellsjökull   Helgrindur   Vegamót   55   Snæfellsnes   Baula

National Park   Hólsfjall   Peninsula

Snæfellsjökull   Búðir   Harfursfell   Heggstaðir   Hraunsnef   Hallmundarhraun

Hellnar   Breiðavík   Eldborg   Fljótstunga   Eiríksjökull   35

Haffjörður   Munaðarnes   Húsafell

Faxaflói   Svignaskarð   Hraunfossar   Langjökull   Hvítárvatn

Borgarnes   Hvanneyri   Geitlandsjökull

Álftanes   Hafnarfjall   Þórisjökull

Borgarfjörður   Saurbær   F338   Sandvatn

Hvalfjörður   Glymur   Bjarnarfell

Akranes   Þingvellir   Gullfoss

Kistufell   Skálabrekka   National Park   Geysir   Háifoss

Mosfellsbær   36   Laugarvatn   37   Bratthólt   Hraun

REYKJAVÍK ✪   Mjóavatn   Apavatn   Reykholt   Græne

Hafnarfjordhur   Nesjavellir   Flúðir   30   Hjálparfoss

Keflavík   Keilir   Hengill   Árnes   Búrfell

Reykjanes-   Hveragerði   Brjánsstaðir   Hekla   Na

Hafnir   Vogar   fólkvangur   Selfoss   Res

43   Ólfusá   Laugaland   F210

Grindavík   Kleifarvatn   Eyrarbakki   Vatnsholt   Hella   Tindfjallajökul

Þorlákshöfn   Hvolsvöllur   Fljótsdalur   Tindfjöll

Mýrdalsj

Seljalandsfoss   Eyjafjallajökul

Ásólfsskáli   Skóga

Heimaey   Skógar   Petu

Vestmannaeyjar   Skeidflotu

NORTH   Islands
ATLANTIC
OCEAN

5 West Iceland
Spectacular vistas and intriguing detours along a fjord-serrated coastline.   **1–2 DAYS**

1 The Golden Circle & the Southwest
An ancient parliament and striking natural wonders.   **2–3 DAYS**

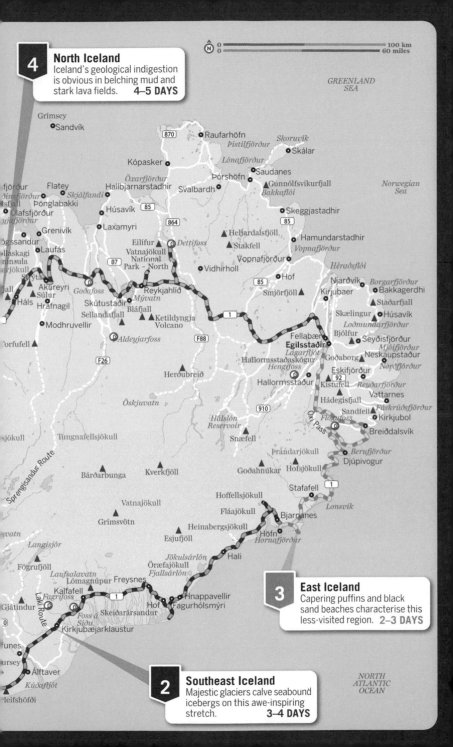

4
North Iceland
Iceland's geological indigestion is obvious in belching mud and stark lava fields. **4–5 DAYS**

3
East Iceland
Capering puffins and black sand beaches characterise this less-visited region. **2–3 DAYS**

2
Southeast Iceland
Majestic glaciers calve seabound icebergs on this awe-inspiring stretch. **3–4 DAYS**

ICELAND'S RING
ROAD

HIGHLIGHTS

★

Jökulsárlón (above) A ghostly procession of luminous blue icebergs drifts serenely through the 25-sq-km Jökulsárlón lagoon before floating out to sea. See it on Trip 2

Skaftafell (left) A gem in the expansive Vatnajökull National Park, Skaftafell encompasses a spellbinding wilderness of glaciers, volcanoes and mountains. See it on Trip 2

Reykjavík (right) A vibrant cultural hub, the capital boasts music, museums, shopping, interesting architecture and a staggering number of coffeehouses serving designer microbrews. See it on Trip 5

CITY GUIDE

REYKJAVÍK

Although tiny in size, Reykjavík has a huge cultural presence. Imaginative Reykjavikers embrace their sense of community and bring a joy to life, creating captivating museums, cool music, and offbeat cafes and bars. The city is also a superb base for touring Iceland's natural wonders: glacier-topped volcanoes, shimmering falls and black-sand beaches.

Harpa concert hall (p77)

Getting Around

You won't need the car in Reykjavík. Walking is the best way to see the compact centre, and there's excellent bus coverage around the whole town.

Parking

Street parking downtown is limited and costs kr250 per hour in the 'Red Zone', kr125 per hour in the 'Blue Zone' and kr90 per two hours in the 'Green Zone'. These charges apply between 9am and 6pm weekdays and 10am to 4pm Saturday.

Where to Eat

Little Reykjavík has an astonishing assortment of eateries. Loads of seafood and Icelandic or New Nordic restaurants serve tried-and-true variations on local fish and lamb, but the capital is also the main spot for finding international eats.

Where to Stay

Reykjavík has loads of accommodation, with hostels, midrange guesthouses (often with shared bathrooms and kitchen) and business-class hotels galore, and top-end boutique hotels and apartments seem to be opening daily. June through August accommodation books out entirely; reservations are essential. Prices are high.

Useful Websites

Visit Reykjavík (www.visitreykjavik.is) Official site for the capital.

Icelandic Road Administration (www.road.is) Details road openings and current conditions.

Lonely Planet (www.lonelyplanet.com/iceland) Destination information, traveller forum and more.

REYKJAVÍK

For more, check out our city and country guides.
www.lonelyplanet.com

TOP EXPERIENCES

➡ **Old Reykjavík**
Explore this historic quarter and shopping in nearby Laugavegur and the capital's many design boutiques.

➡ **National Museum**
Learn about Iceland's settlement and fascinating history.

➡ **Old Harbour Dining**
The Old Harbour is loaded with eating options, from excellent hamburgers and fish and chips to elegant Matur go Drykkur, the gourmet highlight of the bunch.

➡ **Hallgrímskirkja**
Photograph the striking exterior then zip up for sweeping views from the heights of this landmark's modernist steeple.

➡ **Whale-Watching**
Sight the whales leaping off Iceland's shores on an excursion from the Old Harbour.

➡ **Reykjavík Art Museum – Hafnarhús**
Check out contemporary art from installations to paintings and sculpture at this well-curated art magnet.

➡ **Settlement Exhibition**
Peruse a Viking longhouse and artefacts from Reykjavík's first days.

➡ **Harpa**
Enjoy a performance or simply be dazzled by the shiny surfaces and gorgeous interior of Reykjavík's iconic concert hall.

➡ **Party**
Join the *djammið*, a wild pub crawl through heaving nightspots like Kaffibarinn.

➡ **Cafes**
Sidle up to cool cats sipping coffee at quirky cafes.

NEED TO KNOW

CURRENCY
Icelandic króna (kr or ISK)

LANGUAGE
Icelandic; English widely spoken

VISAS
Generally not required for stays of up to 90 days.

FUEL
Petrol stations are regularly spaced but check the distance to the next station when in the highlands. At research, fuel cost about kr205/L.

HIRE CARS
Some of the numerous car-hire companies:

Átak (www.atak.is)

Europcar (www.europcar.is) The biggest company.

Geysir (www.geysir.is)

SADcars (www.sadcars. com) Older fleet, often cheaper prices.

IMPORTANT NUMBERS
Make sure you get a breakdown number from your rental provider.

Emergency Services (☎112)

Road condition information (☎1777)

Weather forecast (☎902 0600) Press 1 after the introduction.

Climate

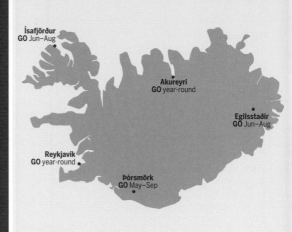

Mild summers, cold winters

Ísafjörður GO Jun–Aug

Akureyri GO year-round

Egilsstaðir GO Jun–Aug

Reykjavík GO year-round

Þórsmörk GO May–Sep

When to Go

High Season (Jun–Aug)
» Visitors descend en masse, especially to Reykjavík and the south. Prices peak; prebookings are essential.

» Endless daylight, plentiful festivals, busy activities.

» Highland mountain roads open to 4WDs, from mid-June or later; hikers welcome.

Shoulder (May & Sep)
» Breezier weather; occasional snows in the highlands (access via mountain roads weather dependent).

» Optimal visiting conditions if you prefer fewer crowds and lower prices over cloudless days.

Low Season (Oct–Apr)
» Mountain roads closed; some minor roads shut due to weather conditions.

» Winter activities on offer, including skiing, snowshoeing, visiting ice caves.

» Brief spurts of daylight; long nights with possible Northern Lights viewings.

Daily Costs

Budget: less than kr18,000
» Camping: kr1200–1800
» Dorm bed: kr4500–7000
» Grill-bar grub or soup lunch: kr1500–2200

Midrange: kr18,000–35,000
» Guesthouse double room: kr18,000–28,000
» Cafe meal: kr2500–3500
» Small vehicle rental (per day): from kr10,000

Top end: more than kr35,000
» Boutique double room: kr30,000–40,000
» Main dish in top-end restaurant: kr4000–7000
» 4WD rental (per day): from kr20,000

Eating

Accommodation In rural areas, guesthouses and hotels may offer meals.

Cafes Open usually from lunchtime into evening, serving simple fare.

Grill bars Often found at petrol stations. Standby for hot dogs and burgers, plus simple soup, fish and lamb dishes.

Restaurants Across the country, the emphasis is on farm-fresh, local produce.

Vegetarians No problem in Reykjavík. Elsewhere around the country there's usually at least one veggie item on menus, but it's often boring.

Sleeping

Hotels From small, bland and business-like to designer dens with all the trimmings.

Guesthouses Run the gamut from homestyle B&Bs to large hotel-like properties.

Hostels Popular budget options across the country.

Campgrounds No requirement to book. Exposure to the elements. Campervans increasingly popular.

Arriving in Iceland

Keflavík International Airport
Bus Public buses (kr1680) and door-to-door shuttle bus companies (kr2100–2700) run the 48km into Reykjavík.

Car Can be rented from the airport; prebook.

Taxis Not heavily utilised due to efficient buses and high cost (kr15,000).

Mobile Phones

Mobile (cell) coverage is widespread. Visitors with GSM phones can roam; a local SIM card with data package is the cheapest option if staying a few days.

Internet Access

Wi-fi is available in most accommodation and eating venues, and in petrol stations.

Money

Iceland is virtually cashless: cards reign supreme, even in rural reaches. ATMs in all towns.

Tipping

Service and VAT taxes are included in prices, so tipping isn't required. Rounding up the bill at restaurants or leaving a small tip for good service is appreciated.

Useful Websites

Visit Iceland (www.visiticeland.com) Iceland's official tourism portal.

Visit Reykjavík (www.visitreykjavik.is) Official site.

Icelandic Met Office (http://en.vedur.is) Best resource for weather forecasts.

Safe Travel (www.safetravel.is) Stay safe while travelling.

Reykjavík Grapevine (www.grapevine.is) Great English-language newspaper and website.

Opening Hours

In general hours increase June to August; many places close in winter. Standard opening hours:

Banks 9am–4pm Monday to Friday

Petrol stations 8am–10pm or 11pm

Restaurants 11.30am–2.30pm and 6pm–9pm or 10pm

Shops 10am–6pm Monday to Friday, 10am–4pm Saturday

Supermarkets 9am–8pm (11pm in Reykjavík)

Vínbúðin (government-run alcohol stores) Variable; many outside Reykjavík only open a couple of hours per day.

For more, see Road Trip Essentials (p118).

Plan Your Trip
Ring Road Planner

Unless you've visited Iceland before, you'll likely struggle to name an Icelandic town besides Reykjavík. You may worry about planning your visit when so much of the country is vast and unknown. Fear not, the path is clear: take the Ring Road.

Best Ring Road Detours

Snæfellsnes Peninsula
A veritable ring road unto itself that takes in lava fields, wild coastline and an infamous ice cap; 200km detour.

Tröllaskagi Peninsula
Follow Rte 76/Rte 82 as it climbs up towards the Arctic – hair-raising road tunnels and scenic panoramas await; 90km detour.

Borgarfjörður Eystri
Take Rte 94 through rhyolite cliffs and down into this quiet hamlet where there are visiting puffins and superb hiking trails; 150km detour.

Vestmannaeyjar
Hop on the ferry at Landeyjahöfn to discover a rugged archipelago of islets; 30km detour plus a 30-minute boat ride each way.

Þórsmörk
Park at Seljalandsfoss and take the bus into a forested kingdom rife with scenic walks; 50km detour along a rutty road accessible only by certified vehicles; hiking also an option.

The 'Diamond Circle'
Dreamed up by marketers, the Diamond Circle barrels north from Mývatn to take in the whale-filled bay of Húsavík; the grand canyon and trails of Ásbyrgi; and the roaring falls at Dettifoss; 180km detour.

Route 1

Route 1 (Þjóðvegur 1), known as the Ring Road, is the country's main thoroughfare, comprising a super-scenic 1330km (830 miles) of mostly paved highway. It's rarely more than one lane in either direction. Countless gems line its path, while secondary roads lead off it to further adventures.

When to Go

The Ring Road is generally accessible year-round (there may be exceptions during winter storms); many of the secondary roads are closed during the colder months. Check out www.road.is for details of road closures, and www.vedur.is for weather forecasts.

Clockwise or Anticlockwise

It doesn't matter which way you tackle the Ring Road – the landscape reveals itself in an equally cinematic fashion from both directions.

If you're travelling during the latter part of summer (August into September), we recommend driving the loop in a clockwise manner – check off your northern must-sees first as warmer weather sticks around a tad longer in the south.

➡ Don't confuse the Ring Road, which loops the country, with the Golden Circle (a tourist route in the country's southwest).

➡ The Ring Road doesn't traverse Iceland's highlands – if you're keen to see more, two highland routes cut through the centre. These roads are only open in summer, and only to 4WDs; happily, all-terrain buses traverse the routes in summer.

How Long Do I Need?

Driving the Ring Road without stopping (or breaking the speed limit) would take about 16 hours. Thus, a week-long trip around the country means an average of about 2½ hours of driving per day. While this might seem a bit full-on, remember that the drive is extraordinarily scenic and in summer there's plenty of daylight.

We recommend a minimum of 10 days to do justice to the Ring Road (two weeks is better). For travellers planning an itinerary that's less than a week, we suggest committing to one or two regions in detail (eg Reykjavík and the south or west; or a week in the north), rather than trying to hoof it around the island.

By Car

Discovering Iceland by private vehicle is by far the most convenient way to go, though it is the most expensive option.

Renting a Car

It's best to start planning early if searching for low rates. The internet is your best resource, but ensure that the name of your rental service appears on your booking, and double-check that all fees are included in the quoted price.

Book early for summer hires – companies sometimes run out of vehicles.

2WD or 4WD?

A 2WD vehicle is fine if you're planning to drive just the Ring Road and major secondary roads. If you want to explore the highlands (driving on 'F' mountain roads), you'll need a 4WD – alternatively, hire a 2WD and book bus trips or super-Jeep tours to less-accessible areas.

For winter, we don't recommend small 2WDs; consider a 4WD for safety (rental prices are considerably lower in winter). Snow tyres are fitted to winter rentals.

Breaking up the Journey

When travelling the Ring Road, use it as a conduit to explore memorable detours. We recommend choosing five mini-bases along the journey to break up the drive. Try selecting one stop in each region through which the Ring Road passes: the west, north, east, southeast and southwest. You could spend several nights at each base, engaging in the area's best activities and detours before moving on.

By Bus

Far less convenient than car rental, Iceland's limited bus service is the most cost-effective option for solo travellers. You should budget double the time of a private vehicle to loop around, lest you spend the majority of the trip staring at the countryside through a window.

For comparison, a bus pass that carries two travellers around the island roughly equals the price (excluding petrol) of a small rental car for a week.

By Bicycle

We don't want to dash your dreams, but cyclists will have a tougher time than expected travelling the Ring Road. The changeable weather makes for tough going, and although the path is mostly paved, there is hardly any room on the shoulder of the road to provide a comfortable distance from vehicular traffic. Cycling can be a great way to explore more-rural regions.

By Hitching & Ridesharing

The most cost-effective way to venture around the Ring Road is to stick out your thumb. In summer it's quite easy to hitch all the way around the Ring Road but be aware of the potential risks involved.

Many hostels have ride-share posterboards in their lobbies. A great resource is www.samferda.is, an online ride-share messageboard.

Outdoor Adventures

PATREKSFJÖRÐUR

A laid-back base for exploring the Westfjords' southern peninsulas: crowded bird cliffs at Látrabjarg, beaches like rosy Rauðasandur and the bike-friendly Þingeyri Peninsula.

ÍSAFJÖRÐUR

Stay in or around the Westfjords' largest town to access Hornstrandir (p116), the kayak-friendly fjords of Ísafjarðardjúp and the rugged central peninsulas.

SNÆFELLSNES PENINSULA

A gorgeous sampler of all that Iceland has to offer: hiking trails, horse riding, hot springs, boat trips, puffins and whales, plus the peninsula's namesake glacier. (p68)

KERLINGARFJÖLL

The highlands region is all about 4WD trails to remote hiking; this mountain range is a hiker's paradise of geothermal wonders and multihued rhyolite mountains.

REYKJAVÍK

The hub of countless tours and adventure trips into the hinterlands, with a focus on the south and west, and of course, the Golden Circle. (p74)

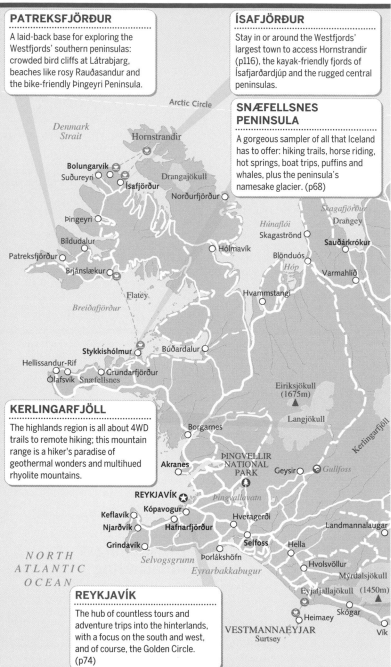

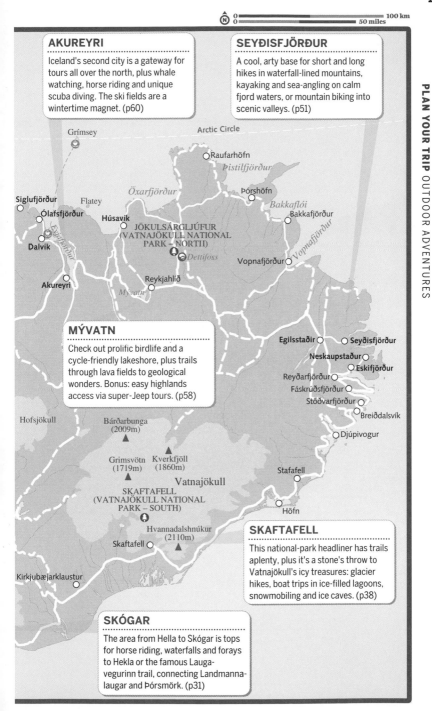

AKUREYRI

Iceland's second city is a gateway for tours all over the north, plus whale watching, horse riding and unique scuba diving. The ski fields are a wintertime magnet. (p60)

SEYÐISFJÖRÐUR

A cool, arty base for short and long hikes in waterfall-lined mountains, kayaking and sea-angling on calm fjord waters, or mountain biking into scenic valleys. (p51)

MÝVATN

Check out prolific birdlife and a cycle-friendly lakeshore, plus trails through lava fields to geological wonders. Bonus: easy highlands access via super-Jeep tours. (p58)

SKAFTAFELL

This national-park headliner has trails aplenty, plus it's a stone's throw to Vatnajökull's icy treasures: glacier hikes, boat trips in ice-filled lagoons, snowmobiling and ice caves. (p38)

SKÓGAR

The area from Hella to Skógar is tops for horse riding, waterfalls and forays to Hekla or the famous Lauga-vegurinn trail, connecting Landmanna-laugar and Þórsmörk. (p31)

Krossneslaug

Hofsós

Selárdalslaug

Pollurinn

Drangsnes

Mývatn
Nature Baths

Egilsstaðir

Lýsuhólslaug

Laugarvatn

REYKJAVÍK

Flúðir

Hveragerði

Landmannalaugar

Blue
Lagoon

2 WEEKS Hot-Pot Hop

Slap on those swim trunks and enjoy Iceland's favourite pastime: wading in warm, mineral-rich hot springs that soothe both the body and the mind. Hop across this geothermic kingdom, dipping your toes in at each source.

Start in **Reykjavík** and do as the locals do – bring your backstroke and some gossip to share at the public pools.

Next, try the **Blue Lagoon**, the Disneyland of swimming spots, and slather rich silica over your face.

Pause in **Hveragerði**, southeast of Reykjavík and one of Iceland's most geothermally active areas – bubbling water abounds.

Head to **Landmannalaugar**, where a steaming stream is the perfect cure-all after some serious hiking.

Cruise by **Flúðir** and see just who else is in on the secret of the natural, meadow-surrounded lagoon.

Swing through mod Fontana, in **Laugarvatn**, for its naturally occurring geyser-sauna (you'll see!).

Soak in **Lýsuhólslaug** and emerge from the algae soup with baby-soft skin.

Scout out **Pollurinn**, just outside of Tálknafjörður – a favourite local hang-out.

Blink and you'll miss the roadside hot-pots in **Drangsnes**, built into a sea wall.

Bask in the otherworldly beauty at **Krossneslaug**, set along the wild, pebble-strewn shore.

Check out stunning **Hofsós**, with near-infinity views from its fjordside pool, plus the chance to book a midnight float.

The north's mellower version of the Blue Lagoon is found at **Mývatn Nature Baths**.

Finish up at **Selárdalslaug**, tucked between two hillocks near Vopnafjörður. Then fly back to Reykjavík from **Egilsstaðir**.

Top: Gamla Laugin, Flúðir (p29)
Bottom: Reykjadalur hot river, Hveragerði

1. Arctic fox **2.** Seal pup **3.** Humpback whale
4. Puffins

EMKA74/SHUTTERSTOCK ©

Wildlife Watching

Iceland's magical natural realm is the playground for some headlining acts, including breaching whales, basking seals, elusive Arctic foxes and bumper birdlife (the scene stealer: cute, clownish puffins, of course). The support cast of wandering sheep and wild-maned horses are still impossibly photogenic against a cinematic, mountainous backdrop.

The birdlife in Iceland is abundant, especially during the warmest months when migrating species arrive to nest. On coastal cliffs and islands around the country, you can see a mind-boggling array of seabirds. Posted coastal hikes offer access to some of the most populous bird cliffs in the world – don't miss a chance to cavort with puffins.

Whale watching has become one of Iceland's most cherished pastimes – boats depart throughout the year (limited service in the colder months) to catch a glimpse of these lurking beasts as they spray the air. The northern waters around Húsavík and Akureyri are a haven for feeding creatures (usually minke and fin species); travellers who are short on time can hop a boat that departs directly from downtown Reykjavík (p78). In winter, it's possible to see orcas crash through the frigid waters – the best point of departure is the Snæfellsnes Peninsula (p68).

BEST WILDLIFE-WATCHING SPOTS

Vestmannaeyjar Islands (p32) Zoom between islets as you snap photos of a *Peterson Field Guide's* worth of birdlife.

Borgarfjörður Eystri It's like you've died and gone to puffin heaven northeast of Egilsstaðir (p51), where encounters with these clumsy birds are up close and personal.

Húsavík (p58) Sample Iceland's original flavour of whale watching at this charming fishing village. There are tours aplenty, especially in summer.

Road Trips

Fjaðrárgljúfur canyon (p36)
KAVRAM/SHUTTERSTOCK ©

The Golden Circle & the Southwest

1

From black-sand Atlantic beaches, spouting geysers and glacier-fed waterfalls to brooding volcanoes and glittering ice caps, this remarkable region is waiting to awe you.

TRIP HIGHLIGHTS

40 km

Þingvellir
Continental plates part at this historic parliament site

START
REYKJAVÍK

Reykholt

3

100 km

Geysir
Ooh and aah as water shoots skywards from the earth

Hella

266 km

Sólheimajökull
Pose for photos at this sparkling glacier tongue

7

8
FINISH

Reynisfjara
Marvel at black basalt columns, sea stacks and rocky buttes

294 km

**2–3 DAYS
294KM /
182 MILES**

GREAT FOR...

BEST TIME TO GO

June to August is busy, but offers the best weather.

ESSENTIAL PHOTO

Black-sand beach at Reynisfjara with basalt-columned cliffs and puffins.

BEST FOR OUTDOORS

Hop between waterfalls cascading from volcanoes and ice caps along the Ring Road.

The Golden Circle & the Southwest

1

The beautiful Golden Circle and Southwest has many of Iceland's most legendary natural wonders, and the further you go the better it gets. Tourist faves, such as the earth-rending parliament at Þingvellir, are just beyond the capital. Churning seas lead to the Vestmannaeyjar archipelago. Then, at the region's far reaches, you'll discover the powerful Hekla and Eyjafjallajökull volcanoes, busy Skógar and Vík, and the hidden valleys of Þórsmörk and Landmannalaugar.

TRIP HIGHLIGHT

1 Þingvellir (p96)
Driving out of Reykjavík along the Ring Road through the capital's northern suburbs, mountains roll into view and the vistas expand. Turn east on Rte 36, passing through lush meadows marbled by clear streams to reach the dramatic rift valley of **Þingvellir National Park** (www.thing vellir.is). One of the iconic stops on the Golden Circle route, Þingvellir is Iceland's most impor-

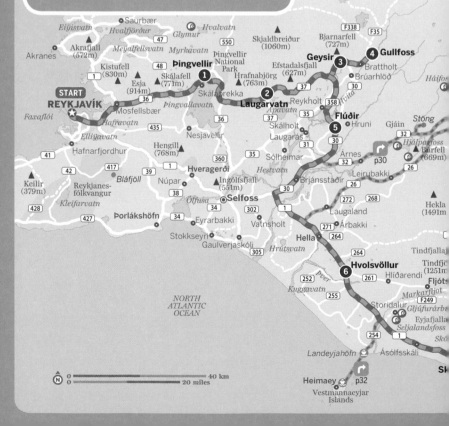

tant historical site and a place of vivid beauty. The Vikings established the world's first democratic parliament, the Alþingi (pronounced ál-thingk-ee, also called Alþing), here in AD 930. The meetings were conducted outdoors and, as with many Saga sites, only the stone foundations of ancient encampments called **búðir** (literally 'booths') remain. The site has a superb natural setting, in an immense, fissured rift valley, caused by the meeting of the North American and Eurasian **tectonic plates**, with rivers and waterfalls. Filling much of the rift plain south of the site, **Þingvallavatn** is Iceland's largest lake, at 84 sq km.

From the **Þingvellir Visitors Centre** (✆482 3613; ⏱9am-6:30pm Apr-Oct, to 5pm Nov-Mar) on Rte 36, at the top of **Almannagjá rift**, follow the path from the outlook down to the **Lögberg** (Law Rock; where the Alþingi convened annually) and the only standing structures in the great rift: a summerhouse and a small **church** dating from 1859. You can also approach the waterfall **Öxarárfoss** from a parking area on Rte 36, and hike down into the rift valley from there. Or park on the eastern edge of the site (Rte 361)

The Drive » This 32km drive begins by tracing the edge of the foothills along Þingvallavatn lake. You'll start on Rte 36, but turn east on Rte 365 to cut south of the dramatic mountains and emerge at Laugarvatn, both a lake and a village of the same name.

---

❷ Laugarvatn (p97)

Laugarvatn (Hot Springs Lake) is fed not only by streams running from the misty fells behind it, but by the hot spring Vígðalaug, famous since medieval times. A village, also called Laugarvatn, sits on the lake's western shore in the lap of the foothills. It is one of the better places to take a break in the Golden Circle. Unwind at **Fontana** (✆486 1400; www.fontana. is; Hverabraut 1; adult/child kr3800/2000; ⏱10am-11pm early Jun-late Aug, 11am-10pm late Aug-early Jun), a swanky lakeside soaking spot boasting three mod wading pools, and a cedar-lined steam room that's fed by a naturally occurring vent below. The cafe has lake views. Or, if you're on a budget, hop into the municipal **geothermal pool** (✆486 1251; Hverabraut 2; adult/child kr500/250; ⏱10am-10pm Mon-Fri, to 6pm Sat & Sun Jun–mid-Aug, reduced hours mid-Aug–May) next door.

TOP TIP:
BOOK AHEAD FOR LODGING

It is absolutely essential to book well ahead for the summer season and on holidays, especially the further south you are going. There is simply not enough accommodation for the number of visitors, and hotels and guesthouses are booked solid. It is not necessary to reserve ahead for campgrounds.

The restaurant **Lindin** (📞486 1262; www.laugarvatn. is; Lindarbraut 2; restaurant mains kr3800-6300, bistro mains kr2200-5600; ⊙noon-10pm May-Sep, reduced hours Oct-Apr) is one of the best in the region and has both a casual bistro and a fine-dining lake-view wing in a sweet little silver house. For afters, get homemade ice cream while looking through viewing windows into the dairy barn at **Efstidalur II** (📞486 1186; www.efstidalur. is; Efstidalur 2; mains kr2250-5500; ⊙7.30am-9.30am & 11.30am-9pm) farm, 12km northeast of town.

The Drive » Leave Laugarvatn to the north along scenic Rte 37, which will wind you away from the lakeside foothills into increasingly open agricultural plains and then join up with Rte 35 to Geysir. As you approach Geysir (29km in total), you'll see first a geothermal outlet venting steam and then the ochre-seared Haukadalur geothermal area around the geyser.

TRIP HIGHLIGHT

❸ Geysir (p97)

One of Iceland's most famous tourist attractions, **Geysir** (gay-zeer; literally 'gusher') is the original hot-water spout after which all other geysers are named. The Great Geysir has been active for perhaps 800 years, and once gushed water up to 80m into the air. But this geyser goes through periods of lessened activity, which seems to

have been the case since 1916. Earthquakes can stimulate activity, but eruptions are rare. Luckily for visitors, the very reliable geyser, **Strokkur**, sits alongside. You rarely have to wait more than five to 10 minutes for the hot spring to shoot an impressive 15m to 30m plume before vanishing down its enormous hole.

The undulating, hissing geothermal area containing Geysir and Strokkur was free to enter at the time of writing, though there is discussion of instituting a fee. The large **Geysir Center** (📞480 6800; www.geysir center.com; ⊙10am-10pm Jun-Aug, to 6pm Sep-May; 🅿🛜♿) across the street from the geysers holds a massive restaurant-cafe and a shopping complex.

The Drive » As you drive this short hop of only 10km along Rte 35 northeast to Gullfoss, stop and look back at the geothermal geyser area for a chance at great photos. Then follow the road as it dips the vast, almost hidden, canyon of the Hvítá river north to the falls.

----

❹ Gullfoss (p97)

Iceland's most famous waterfall, **Gullfoss** (Golden Falls; www.gullfoss.is) is a spectacular double cascade dropping a dramatic 32m in the Hvítá river. As it descends, it kicks up brilliant walls of spray before thundering down a rocky ravine. On sunny days the mist creates

shimmering rainbows, while in winter the falls glitter with ice. Although it's a popular sight, the remote location still makes you feel the forces of nature that have worked this landscape for millennia. Above the falls there's a small tourist information centre, shop and cafe.

If you'd like to approach the falls on horseback, book in with **Geysir Hestar** (📞847 1046; www. geysirhestar.com; Kjóastaðir 2; one-/two-/three-hour rides kr9500/12,500/17,000), which offers horse riding for all skill levels and has one route along the river canyon to the falls. There are also opportunities for river rafting downriver from the falls with **Arctic Rafting** (📞571 2200; www. arcticrafting.com; ⊙mid-May–mid-Sep), operating out of Drumboddsstaðir, or with **Iceland Riverjet** (📞863 4506; www.icelandriverjet.com; Skólabraut 4; ⊙mid-Apr–Sep) in Reykholt.

The Drive » The easiest route to Flúðir (35km) is to retrace your drive along Rte 35 to the junction with Rte 37, then turn south on Rte 35 along the western bank of the Hvítá, crossing the river on Rte 359 and continuing into Flúðir. Find Gamla Laugin lagoon signposted on the northern bank of the river Litla-Laxá in Flúðir.

----

❺ Flúðir (p98)

Little agrarian Flúðir is known throughout Iceland for its geothermal greenhouses that grow the majority of the country's mushrooms, and it's also a popular weekend getaway for Reykjavikers with private cottages. More recently it's a super stop for its beautifully refurbished hot springs, **Gamla Laugin** (Secret Lagoon; ☏555 3351; www.secret lagoon.is; adult/child kr2800/ free; ☺10am-10pm May-Sep, noon-8pm Oct-Apr). Soak in this broad, calm geothermal pool, mist rising and ringed by natural rocks. The walking trail along the edge of this lovely hot spring passes the local river and a series of sizzling vents and geysers. Surrounding meadows fill with wildflowers in summer. Increasingly popular, the lagoon gets packed with tour bus crowds in mid-afternoon, so come early or late in the day.

To sample some of the local produce, stop in at **Efra Sel Farmers Market** about 3km northwest of town, near the golf course on Rte 359. It offers the best produce of the region: veggies, meat, strawberries, rhubarb pie and bread, plus it has picnic tables out front.

The Drive » This 66km drive takes you south on Rte 30 for 31km to rejoin the Ring Road, where you then turn east to the small town of Hvolsvöllur. Driving out of Flúðir, the terrain becomes dramatic, with rock buttes rising from green plains.

TOURING THE HIGHLANDS

Landmannalaugar

Mind-blowing multicoloured mountains, soothing hot springs, rambling lava flows and clear blue lakes make Landmannalaugar one of Iceland's most unique destinations, and a must for explorers of the highlands. It's a favourite with Icelanders and visitors alike...as long as the weather cooperates. Part of the **Fjallabak Nature Reserve**, Landmannalaugar (600m above sea level) includes the largest geothermal field in Iceland outside the Grímsvötn caldera in Vatnajökull. Its multihued peaks are made of rhyolite – a mineral-filled lava that cooled unusually slowly, causing amazing colours. The area is the official starting point for the famous multiday **Laugavegurinn hike** to Þórsmörk, and there's excellent day hiking as well.

Þórsmörk

The hidden valley of Þórsmörk (*thors*-mork, literally 'Thor's Forest') sits at the confluence of several larger river-carved valleys. A nature reserve, Þórsmörk is a verdant realm of forest and flower-filled lees that looks onto curling gorges, icy rivers and three looming glaciers (Tindfjallajökull, Eyjafjallajökull and Mýrdalsjökull). The glaciers protect this quiet spot from some of the region's harsher weather; it is often warmer or drier in Þórsmörk than nearby.

Getting There & Away

Landmannalaugar and Þórsmörk may seem relatively close to the Ring Road on a map, but you'll need to take a bus or go by high-clearance 4WD (super-Jeep tour) to ford the rivers on the way to the reserve (or for Þórsmörk you can hike in from Skógar). As you get close to Þórsmörk, for example, you must cross the dangerous Krossá river. Regular 4WDs cannot make it. You'll see that they are parked where people have hitched rides with buses or super-Jeeps. So, the best bet is to ditch your rental car at the Ring Road and catch either a **Reykjavík Excursions** (Kynnisferðir; ☏580 5400; www.re.is; BSÍ Bus Terminal, Vatnsmýrarvegur 10), **Sterna** (☏551 1166; www.sterna.is; Harpa concert hall, Austurbakki 2; ☺7am-midnight Jun-Aug, 8am-10pm Sep-May) or **Trex** (☏587 6000; www.trex.is) bus, or book in with excellent local operators such as **Southcoast Adventure** (☏867 3535; www.southadventure.is) or Midgard Adventure (p30).

❻ Hvolsvöllur (p98)

The farms around Hvolsvöllur were the setting for the bloody events of *Njál's Saga,* one of Iceland's favourites. Today the Saga sites exist mainly as place names or peaceful grassed-over ruins, but you can get a vivid summary of the story at **Sögusetrið** (Saga Centre; ☑487 8781; www.njala.is; Hliðarvegur 14, Hvolsvöllur; adult/child kr900/free; ⊙9am-6pm mid-May–mid-Sep, 10am-5pm Sat & Sun mid-Sep–mid-May), an interactive museum devoted to the dramatic events. Add stitches to an intricate 90m embroidery called Njál's Saga Tapestry in the back room.

Next, visit the medieval turf-roofed farm at **Keldur** (☑530 2200; www.thjodminjasafn.is; kr750; ⊙10am-5pm mid-Jun–mid-Aug), a historic settlement that once belonged to Ingjaldur Höskuldsson, a character in *Njál's Saga*. About 5km west of Hvolsvöllur, unsurfaced Rte 264 winds about 8km north along the Rangárvellir valley to the pastoral site.

In Hvolsvöllur, the new **LAVA – Iceland Volcano & Earthquake Center** (www.lavacentre.is; Austurvegur 14, Hvolsvöllur; adult/child kr2600/free, cinema only kr1200/free; ⊙exhibition 10am-7pm, LAVA house 9am-10pm) opens in spring 2017 with a full-blown multimedia experience immersing you in Iceland's volcanic and seismic life. To get out into this amazing terrain, hook up with **Midgard Adventure** (☑770 2030; www.midgard adventure.is; Dufþaksbraut 14), one of South Iceland's best bespoke adventure operators.

➦ DETOUR: ÞJÓRSÁRDALUR

Start: ❺ Flúðir (p28)

The powerful Þjórsá is Iceland's longest river, a fast-flowing, churning mass of milky glacial water that courses 230km from Vatnajökull down to the Atlantic. Route 32 follows the western side of the river and is easy to join at the junction with Rte 30, just south of Flúðir. As the road moves upstream into the highlands you'll traverse broad plains, split by the enormous river, that lead to volcanic fields and finally the foothills of the mountains beyond.

Stop in briefly at **Þjórsárstofa** (Þjórsá Visitor Centre; ☑486 6115; www.thjorsarstofa.is; ⊙10am-6pm Jun-Aug) in Árnes to see a free film and displays on the region, then continue 26km northeast to the short (1km) signposted track to delightful waterfall **Hjálparfoss**. The azure falls tumble in two chutes over twisted basalt columns and into a deep pool.

Next, make your way out to unique ruins at **Stöng**; a rough 5km dirt road branches off the other side of Rte 32 from Hjálparfoss. Buried by white volcanic ash in 1104 during one of Hekla's eruptions, the ancient farm at Stöng once belonged to Gaukur Trandilsson, a 10th-century Viking. Excavated in 1939 (Iceland's first proper archaeological dig), it's an important site, used to help date Viking houses elsewhere.

A path from Stöng takes you a couple of kilometres to the lush little valley of **Gjáin**, full of twisting lava, otherworldly caves and spectacular waterfalls. It was a filming location in *Game of Thrones*.

From Stöng you can also walk or take a 4WD 9km northeast along a track to Iceland's second-highest waterfall, **Háifoss**, which plunges 122m off the edge of a plateau into an undulating lava canyon.

Traverse the surreal black-stone river delta to Rte 26 to drive south and rejoin the Ring Road. Rte 26 passes alongside **Hekla**, one of Iceland's most ominous volcanoes.

Skógafoss

The Drive » After Hvolsvöllur, loop east for 49km on the Ring Road to Skógar. The drive brings you through broad plains carved by rivers and along the base of hulking Eyjafjallajökull, made famous with its ashy 2010 explosion. Views are magnificent on clear days: the ice caps of Eyjafjallajökull and Tindfjallajökull inland, and the Vestmannaeyjar Islands offshore. Stop 22km along the way at thundering waterfall, Seljalandsfoss.

TRIP HIGHLIGHT

7 Skógar (p98)

Skógar nestles under the **Eyjafjallajökull** ice cap just north of the Ring Road. This little tourist settlement is the start (or occasionally end) of the hike over the **Fimmvörðuháls Pass** to Þórsmörk, and is one of the activities centres of the Southwest. At its western edge, you can see the dizzying 62m waterfall, **Skógafoss**. Climb the steep staircase alongside for giddy views, or walk to the foot of the falls, shrouded in sheets of mist and rainbows. Legend has it that a settler named Þrasi hid a chest of gold behind Skógafoss...

On the eastern side of town, the fantastic

Skógar Folk Museum
(Skógasafn; ☎487 8845;
www.skogasafn.is; adult/child
kr2000/free; ☺9am-6pm
Jun-Aug, 10am-5pm Sep-May),
covers all aspects of
Icelandic life, with extensive exhibits, restored
buildings (a church, a
turf-roofed farmhouse,

cowsheds), and a huge,
modern building containing a transport and communication museum.

From Skógar, it's also
easy to join a guided
walk on one of the easiest
glacial tongues to reach:
Sólheimajökull. This icy
outlet glacier unfurls

from the main **Mýrd-alsjökull** ice cap and is a
favourite spot for glacial
walks and ice climbing.
Route 221 leads 4.2km
off the Ring Road to a
small car park and the
Arcanum Glacier Café
(Café Solheimajökull; ☎547
1500; www.arcanum.is; snacks

DETOUR: VESTMANNAEYJAR ISLANDS

Start: ❻ Hvolsvöllur (p30)

East of Hvolsvöllur, Rte 254 shoots 12km south of the Ring Road to **Landeyjahöfn** where the **ferry** (☎481 2800; www.eimskip.is; adult/child/bicycle/car kr1320/660/660/2120) leaves for the Vestmannaeyjar Islands, which can be visited on a day trip or overnight. Jagged and black, the Vestmannaeyjar (sometimes called the Westman Islands) form 15 eye-catching silhouettes off the southern shore. The islands were formed by submarine volcanoes around 11,000 years ago, except for Surtsey, the archipelago's newest addition, which rose from the waves in 1963.

Heimaey is the only inhabited island and is famous for the 1973 eruption that almost smothered the town. The sheltered harbour lies between dramatic *klettur* (escarpments) and two ominous volcanoes – blood-red **Eldfell** and conical **Helgafell**. Heimaey is also famous for its puffins (around 10 million birds come here to breed); make time to walk, cycle or drive around the island to see them, or take a boat tour with **Ribsafari** (☎661 1810, 846 2798; www.ribsafari.is; Básaskersbryggja 8; 1hr tour per adult/child kr8000/4500, Surtsey tour kr16,500/9500; ☺mid-Apr–Oct) or **Viking Tours** (☎488 4884; www.vikingtours.is; Strandvegur 65; ☺10am-6pm May–mid-Sep).

State-of-the-art volcano museum **Eldheimar** (Pompeii of the North; ☎488 2700; www.eldheimar.is; Gerðisbraut 10; adult/child kr2300/1200; ☺10.30am-6pm May–mid-Oct, 1-5pm Wed-Sun mid-Oct–Apr) is also a must. More than 400 buildings lie buried under lava from the 1973 eruption, and on the edge of the flow this museum revolves around one house excavated from 50m of pumice. The museum allows a glimpse into the home with its crumbling walls and intact but toppled knick-knacks, and is filled with multimedia exhibits on the eruption and its aftermath.

Lovely seaside 15th-century fort **Skansinn** was built to defend the harbour (not too successfully – when Algerian pirates arrived in 1627, they simply landed on the other side of the island).

Kids might enjoy **Sæheimar** (☎481 1997; www.saeheimar.is; Heiðarvegur 12; adult/child kr1200/500; ☺10am-5pm May-Sep, 1-4pm Sat Oct-Apr) aquarium and natural history museum where there's often a teenage puffin wobbling about – the museum is an informal bird hospital.

If time permits, eat at **Slippurinn** (☎481 1515; www.slippurinn.com; Strandvegur 76; lunch kr 2200-3000, dinner kr3500-4000; ☺noon-2.30pm & 5-10pm early May–mid-Sep), one of the best restaurants in Iceland for high-concept Icelandic fare, or grab a bite before your ferry at harbourside **Tanginn** (☎414 4420; www.tanginn.is; Básaskersbryggja 8; mains kr1600-5800).

Reynisdrangur sea stacks

kr750-1375; ⊘9.30am-5pm May-Sep, reduced hours Oct-Apr; 🛜), from where you can walk the 800m to the ice along a track edging the glacial lagoon. Don't attempt to climb onto the glacier unguided – contact **Arcanum** (📱487 1500; www.arcanum.is), **Icelandic Mountain Guides** (📱894 2956; www.mountainguides.is; ⊘9am-6pm) or **Mountain Excursion** (📱897 7737; www.mountainexcursion.is).

The Drive ≫ As the Ring Road arcs 33km east from Skógar to Vík, the haunches of the foothills rise to glaciers, mountaintops and volcanoes inland, while rivers descend from mysterious gorges and course across the broad sweep of pastures to black-sand beaches and the crashing ocean.

- - - - - - - - -

> TRIP HIGHLIGHT

❽ Vík (p99)

The welcoming little community of Vík (aka Vík í Mýrdal) has become a booming hub for a very beautiful portion of the south coast. Iceland's southernmost town, it's also the rainiest, but that doesn't stop the madhouse atmosphere in summer, when every room within 100km is booked solid. On the west side of **Reynisfjall** (340m), the high ridge above Vík, Rte 215 leads 5km down to black-sand beach **Reynisfjara**. It's backed by an incredible stack of basalt columns that look like a magical church organ, and there are outstanding views west to Dyrhólaey. Surrounding cliffs are pocked with caves formed from twisted basalt, and puffins belly flop into the crashing sea during summer. Immediately offshore are the tower-

ing **Reynisdrangur sea stacks**. Tradition says they're masts of a ship that trolls were stealing when they got caught in the sun. At all times watch for rogue waves: people are regularly swept away.

One of the south coast's most recognisable natural formations is the rocky plateau and huge stone sea arch at **Dyrhólaey** (deer-lay), which rises dramatically from the surrounding plain 10km west of Vík, at the end of Rte 218. Visit its crashing black beaches and get awesome views from atop the promontory. The islet is a nature reserve rich in birdlife, including puffins; some or all of it can be closed during nesting season (15 May to 25 June).

Southeast Iceland

2

The mighty Vatnajökull ice cap dominates the Southeast, its huge rivers of frozen ice pouring down steep-sided valleys towards the sea, like icing on a cake. Vistas are vast and otherworldly.

TRIP HIGHLIGHTS

227 km

Route F985
Take a hair-raising snowmobile ride, 840m above sea level

140 km

Skaftafell
The jewel in the crown of Vatnajökull National Park

10 Höfn **FINISH**

8

5

6

192 km

Jökulsárlón
Boat around the ice sculptures of a captivating lagoon

START
Vík

165 km

Ingólfshöfði
Tour an offshore promontory rich in panoramas and birdlife

3–4 DAYS
272KM / 169 MILES

GREAT FOR...

BEST TIME TO GO
Hiking from June to September; ice caves from mid-November to March.

ESSENTIAL PHOTO
The glowing blue icebergs of Jökulsárlón ice lagoon.

BEST FOR FOODIES
Tuck into locally caught langoustine in Höfn.

Jökulsárlón glacier lagoon (p40)

2 Southeast Iceland

The 200km stretch of Ring Road from Kirkjubæjarklaustur to Höfn is mind-blowing, transporting you across stark deltas of grey glacial sand, past lost-looking farms, around the toes of craggy mountains, and alongside glacier tongues and ice-filled lagoons. The only thing you won't pass is a town – but there are properties offering brilliant activities, accommodation and meals (book well ahead, as beds here are in hot demand).

❶ Fjaðrárgljúfur

The route east from Vík is a scenic delight, with the Reynisdrangur sea stacks receding in the rearview mirror while you traverse **Mýrdalssandur** outwash plain, formed from eruptions of the Katla volcano, and then **Eldhraun**, remarkable moss-covered lava fields created by the epic Laki eruptions of 1783.

After about 65km, take the turn north on Rte 206 and follow the road for 3km to reach Fjaðrárgljúfur, a darkly

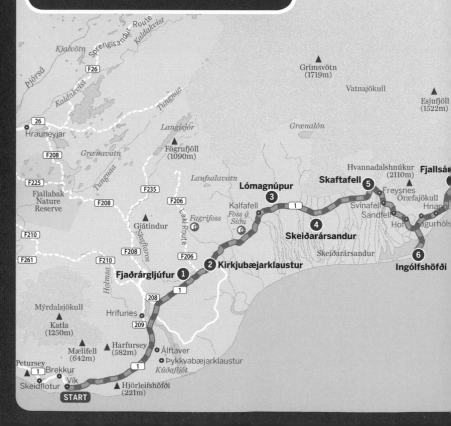

picturesque canyon carved out by the river Fjaðrá. A walking track follows its southern edge for a couple of kilometres, with plenty of places to gaze down into its rocky depths.

The Drive >> Return to the Ring Road and continue east – it's 6km until you reach the junction with Kirkjubæjarklaustur. En route, note the vast, dimpled, vivid-green pseudocrater field (known as Landbrotshólar) south of the Ring Road. Pseudocraters formed when hot lava poured over wetlands; the subsurface water boiled and steam exploded through to make these barrowlike mounds.

❷ Kirkjubæjar-klaustur (p100)

Many a foreign tongue has been tied in knots trying to say Kirkjubæjarklaustur. The name translates as 'church-farm-cloister', and the locals simply call it 'Klaustur' (pronounced like 'cloister'). The town is tiny, even by Icelandic standards – a few houses and farms scattered across a brilliant green backdrop. Still, it's the only real service town between Vík and Höfn, so stop for petrol and groceries, and to explore some cool anomalies and top-notch walks. The basalt columns of **Kirkjugólf**, smoothed down and cemented with moss, were once mistaken for an old church floor rather than a work of nature, and it's easy to see why. The honeycombed slab lies in a field about 400m northwest of the N1 petrol station. At the western end of the village, **Systrafoss** (Sisters' Falls) is a lovely double waterfall. The lake **Systravatn**, a short saunter up the cliffs beside the waterfall, was once a bathing place for nuns.

The Drive >> About 11km from Klaustur you'll pass waterfall Foss á Síðu tumbling down from the cliffs. Just east of the waterfall is the outcrop Dverghamrar (Dwarf Rocks) – two rock formations that feature classic basalt columns and are thought to be the dwelling place of some of Iceland's 'hidden people'. From here the road marches on, past emerald green landscapes interspersed with gravelly riverbeds.

❸ Lómagnúpur (p101)

Adding eye candy to an impressive road trip, a precipitous 767m-tall palisade of cliffs known as Lómagnúpur towers distinctively over the landscape. It's full of legends and looks particularly good as a backdrop to the old turf-roofed farm at **Núpsstaður** just to its

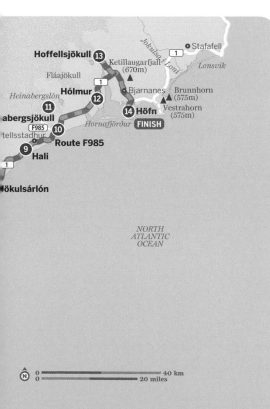

Hoffellsjökull ⑬
Fláajökull
Ketillaugarfjall (670m)
Heinabergslón
Hólmur ⑫
Bjarnanes
Brunnhorn (575m)
Stafafell
Lónsvík
abergsjökull ⑪
F985 ⑩
tellsstadhur
Route F985
⑨
Hali
Jökulsárlón
Hornafjörður ⑭ Höfn **FINISH**
Vestrahorn (575m)

NORTH ATLANTIC OCEAN

Ⓝ 0 ———— 40 km
0 ———— 20 miles

west. The farm buildings date from the early 19th century, and the idyllic chapel is one of Iceland's last turf churches. Note that you can't drive onto the property, but you can park by the road and walk up to the buildings to take photos.

The Drive » As you continue east, you'll encounter Skeiðarársandur, a barren outwash plain stretching some 50km. It's a flat expanse of barren grey-black sands, fierce scouring winds and fast-flowing glacial rivers.

- - - - - - - - - - - -

④ Skeiðarársandur

The sandar are eerily flat and empty regions sprawling along Iceland's southern coast. High in the mountains, glaciers scrape up silt, sand and gravel, which is then carried by glacial rivers or (more dramatically) by glacial bursts down to the coast and dumped in huge, desertlike plains. The sandar here are so impressively huge that the Icelandic word (singular: sandur) is used internationally to describe the topographic phenomenon of a glacial outwash plain.

Skeiðarársandur, the largest sandur in the world, covers a 1300-sq-km area and was formed by the Skeiðarárjökull glacier. Since the Settlement Era, Skeiðarársandur has swallowed a considerable amount of farmland and it continues to grow.

The section of Ring Road that crosses Skeiðarársandur was the last bit of the national highway to be constructed, in 1974 (until then, residents of Höfn had to drive to Reykjavík via Akureyri in the north).

The Drive » As you traverse the sandur, note the long gravel dykes that have been strategically positioned to channel floodwaters. They did little good, however, when in late 1996 three bridges were washed away like matchsticks by a massive *jökulhlaup* (glacial flood). There's a memorial of twisted bridge girders just west of Skaftafell.

- - - - - - - - - - - -

TRIP HIGHLIGHT

⑤ Skaftafell (p101)

Skaftafell, the jewel in the crown of **Vatna-jökull National Park**, encompasses a breath-taking collection of peaks and glaciers. It's the country's favourite wilderness: annually, more than half a million visitors come to marvel at thundering waterfalls, twisted birch woods, the tangled web of rivers threading across the sandar, and the crevass-pleated outlet glaciers flowing down from the immense Vatnajökull ice cap.

The **Skaftafellsstofa Visitor Centre** (☏470 8300; www.vjp.is; ◷9am-7pm May-Sep, 10am-5pm Feb-Apr, Oct & Nov, 11am-5pm Dec, 10am-4pm Jan) has exhibitions and a cafe, and oversees a large campground. Helpful rangers provide maps and information on park attractions and glorious trails; nearby activity companies offer glacier walks and more.

Star of a hundred post-cards, **Svartifoss** (Black Falls) is a stunning, moody-looking waterfall flanked by geometric black basalt columns. It's reached by an easy 1.8km trail leading up from the visitor centre. Another popular option is the easy one-hour return walk (3.7km) to **Skaf-tafellsjökull**. The marked trail begins at the visitor centre and leads to the glacier face.

The Drive » The unfolding landscape of glittering glaciers

TOP TIP:
LOCAL BEER

We're a sucker for a good sales pitch, and Vatnajökull Beer has it in spades: 'frozen in time' beer brewed from 1000-year-old water (ie Jökulsárlón icebergs), flavoured with locally grown Arctic thyme. It's sold in restaurants around the Southeast. Give it a try for its fruity, malty flavour.

Ice cave in Vatnajökull National Park

and brooding mountains makes it difficult to keep your eyes on the road. On clear days, look for the peak of Iceland's highest mountain, Hvannadalshnúkur (2110m). The signposted departure point for Ingólfshöfði tours is about 25km east of Skaftafell at Fagurhólsmýri (drive south to the tour departure hut, 2km off the Ring Road).

---

6 Ingólfshöfði (p102)

While everyone's gaze naturally turns inland in this spectacular part of Iceland, there are reasons to look offshore, too – in particular to the 76m-high Ingólfshöfði

promontory, rising from the flatlands like a strange dream.

In spring and summer, this beautiful, isolated nature reserve is overrun with nesting puffins, skuas and other seabirds. It's also of great historical importance – it was here that Ingólfur Arnarson, Iceland's first settler, stayed the winter on his original foray to the country in AD 874.

Tours of Ingólfshöfði begin with a fun ride across 6km of shallow tidal lagoon (in a tractor-drawn wagon), then a short but steep sandy climb, followed by

a 1½-hour guided walk round the flat headland. The emphasis is on bird-watching, with stunning mountain backdrops to marvel over. Note that puffins usually leave around mid-August. Tours are run by **From Coast to Mountains** (Öræfaferðir; ☑894 0894; www.puffintour.is; tours adult/child kr7500/2500; ⊙ tours 10.15am & 1.30pm Mon-Sat mid-May–mid-Aug). Confirm times via the website, where you can also book tickets.

The Drive » More ice-tinted landscapes await, to fill your 20-minute drive to the next stop.

VATNAJÖKULL NATIONAL PARK

Vast, varied and spectacular, Vatnajökull National Park was founded in 2008, when authorities created a giant megapark by joining the Vatnajökull ice cap with two previously established national parks: Skaftafell in Southeast Iceland and Jökulsárgljúfur in the northeast. With recent additions, the park now measures 13,900 sq km – nearly 14% of the entire country (it's one of the largest national parks in Europe).

The park boundaries encircle a staggering richness of landscapes and some of Iceland's greatest natural treasures, created by the combined forces of rivers, glacial ice, and volcanic and geothermal activity (yes, fire-and-ice cliché alert!). The entirety of the Vatnajökull ice cap is protected, including countless glistening outlet glaciers and glacial rivers. There are incredible waterfalls such as Dettifoss and Svartifoss, the storied Lakagígar crater row, Askja and other volcanoes of the highlands, and an unending variety of areas where geology, ecology and history lessons spring to life.

The park's website (www.vjp.is) is filled with important information – details on trails, campsites, access roads etc, plus it has downloadable maps and brochures. There are useful visitor centres in the Southeast in the towns of Kirkjubæjarklaustur (p100) and **Höfn** (☏470 8330; www.visitvatnajokull.is; Heppuvegur 1; ⊗8am-8pm Jun-Aug, 9am-5pm May & Sep, 9am-1pm Oct-Apr), and at Skaftafell (p101).

Hiking trails and 4WD routes can get you to remote gems, but you don't have to get off the beaten track to sample some of the park's highlights – in fact, quite a few worthy diversions (and awesome vistas) can be accessed from a standard Ring Road journey of the country, and there's a smorgasbord of tour offerings.

- - - - - - - - - - -

❼ Fjallsárlón

A sign on the Ring Road indicates Fjallsárlón. This is an easily accessible glacier lagoon (about 1km off the Ring Road), considerably less famous than busy Jökulsárlón, 10km further east.

If you have the time, stop at both lagoons to admire their different features: Jökulsárlón is much larger and more dramatic, while from Fjallsárlón's shores you can see the glacier snout (icebergs calve from Fjallsjökull outlet glacier). There are lovely walks at each site, and both lagoons offer boat rides. Fjallsárlón wins brownie points for

building a new visitor centre, with cafe. Check out **Fjallsárlón Glacial Lagoon Boat Tours** (☏666 8006; www.fjallsarlon.is; adult/child kr6200/3500; ⊗tours hourly 10am-5pm May–Sep) for information.

The Drive ≫ It's only 10km from Fjallsárlón to Jökulsárlón. The latter sits right beside the Ring Road, and even when you're driving along, expecting this surreal scene, it's still a gorgeous visual surprise. Be careful – there's a single-lane bridge here, and lots of distracted drivers!

- - - - - - - - - - -

`TRIP HIGHLIGHT`

❽ Jökulsárlón (p102)

One of Iceland's most magical sights, Jökulsárlón glacier lagoon is

filled with spectacular, glittering blue icebergs drifting out to sea. You'll be wowed by the wondrous ice sculptures as they spin in the changing light; you can also scout for seals in the lagoon and take a boat trip.

The icebergs calve from Breiðamerkurjökull glacier, an offshoot of Vatnajökull. They can spend up to five years floating in the 25-sq-km-plus, 260m-deep lagoon, melting, refreezing and occasionally toppling over with a mighty splash, startling the birds. They then move on via **Jökulsá**, Iceland's shortest river, out to sea.

Take a memorable 40-minute trip with **Glacier Lagoon Amphibious Boat Tours** (☑478 2222; www.icelagoon.is; adult/child kr5000/1500; ☉9am-7pm Jun-Aug, 10am-5pm Apr, May, Sep & Oct), the vehicles of which trundle along the shore like buses before driving into the water. It also offers Zodiac tours, as does **Ice Lagoon Zodiac Boat Tours** (☑860 9996; www.icelagoon.com; adult/child kr9500/6000; ☉9am-5.30pm mid-May–mid-Sep), which speed up to the glacier edge (not done by the amphibious boats) before cruising back slowly. Check online for details and to book ahead.

The Drive ≫ Before leaving Jökulsárlón, visit the river mouth (there are car parks on the ocean side of the Ring Road), where you'll see ice boulders resting photogenically on the black-sand beach as part of their final journey out to sea. It's only a short hop (14km) from Jökulsárlón to the tiny settlement of Hali.

- - - - - - - - - - - -

❾ Hali (p102)

There's a small cluster of in-demand accommodation at Hali, the closest settlement to Jökulsárlón. Here you'll also find **Þórbergssetur** (☑478 1078; www.thorbergur. is; adult/child kr1000/free; ☉9am-8pm), a cleverly crafted museum (its inspired exterior looks like a shelf of books) that pays tribute to the most famous son of this

sparsely populated region – writer Þórbergur Þórðarson (1888–1974). Þórbergssetur also functions as a kind of cultural centre, with changing art exhibitions and a quality **cafe-restaurant** (www.hali.is/restaurant; mains lunch kr1550-3100, dinner kr3200-5500; ☉11am-9pm) specialising in locally caught Arctic char.

The Drive ≫ The super-scenic stretch of Ring Road between Hali and Höfn is 66km in length, and home to around 20 rural properties (many with glaciers in their backyards) offering accommodation, activities and occasionally food. About 21km east of Hali, the F985 track branches north to the broad glacial spur Skálafellsjökull.

- - - - - - - - - - - -

TRIP HIGHLIGHT

❿ Route F985

This dramatic 16km-long road is practically vertical in places, and is for large 4WDs and confident drivers only. Don't even think of attempting to drive Rte F985 in a 2WD car – you'll end up with a huge rescue bill. Instead, take a ride with one of two companies that drive tourists up the road and then guide them on icy endeavours.

At the end of Rte F985, 840m above sea level and with spectacular 360-degree views, most travellers choose to do an awesome **snowmobile ride**. You're kitted out with overalls, helmets, boots and gloves, and

play follow-the-leader along a fixed trail. It's great fun, but if the ski-doo isn't your thing you can also take a **super-Jeep ride** onto the ice.

Contact **Glacier Jeeps** (☑478 1000, 894 3133; www. glacierjeeps.is; ☉mid-May–mid-Oct), which does pick-up from the small car park at the corner of the Ring Road and Rte F985, or **Glacier Journey** (☑867 0493; www.glacierjourney. is), which operates from **Guesthouse Skálafell** (☑478 1041; www.skalafell.net; d with/without bathroom incl breakfast kr24,500/20,100) in summer; in winter, Glacier Journey's base is at Jökulsárlón.

The Drive ≫ Once back on the Ring Road, you'll pass a turn-off to a cluster of guesthouses, including Guesthouse Skálafell, and then a sign indicating Heinabergsjökull, a glacier tongue reached after 8km on gravel. It pays to ask locally about the condition of the road before setting off in a 2WD.

- - - - - - - - - -

⓫ Heinabergsjökull

Vatnajökull National Park authorities are working with a handful of landowners between Jökulsárlón and Höfn to open up public access to areas of raw natural beauty. These areas are signed off the Ring Road – for now, they are not especially well known, so you stand a good chance of finding yourself a tranquil pocket of glaciated wonder.

Heinabergsjökull has lovely walks, and you can go on brilliant summertime kayaking trips on the icy lagoon (called Heinabergslón) at its snout. The trips are operated by **IceGuide** (661 0900; www.iceguide. is), a company based at Guesthouse Skálafell; the guesthouse also maintains some excellent walking trails in the area, open to all.

The Drive » Rejoin the Ring Road and continue 11km east (past a lookout point) to reach Hólmur.

----

⑫ Hólmur

A perfect pit stop for families, **Hólmur** (478 2063; www.holmurinn.is; s/d without bathroom from kr10,600/13,800) farm offers well-priced farmhouse accommodation and a sweet **farm zoo** (adult/child kr800/600; May-Sep) with an abundance of feathered and furry friends. Also here is a stand-out restaurant, **Jón Ríki** (478 2063; www. jonriki.is; mains lunch kr1390-2590, dinner kr2390-6490;

11.30am-2pm Jun-late Aug, 6-9.30pm year-round).

The glacier tongue **Fláajökull** is 8km off the Ring Road on a gravel road, signposted east of Hólmur. A great walking trail leads from the parking area to the glacial tongue. Glacier walks are operated on Fláajökull, led by **Glacier Trips** (779 2919; www. glaciertrips.is) – this is a great alternative to Skaftafell-area glacier walks, as Fláajökull sees few tourists.

ICY ACTIVITIES

Activities that explore Vatnajökull's icy vastness – glacier walks, super-Jeep tours, lagoon boat tours and snowmobile safaris – are accessed along the Ring Road between Skaftafell and Höfn.

Glacier Walks

It's utterly liberating to strap on crampons and crunch your way around a glacier. But as magnetic as the glaciers are, they are also riven with fissures and are potentially dangerous, so don't be tempted to stride out onto one without the right equipment and guiding.

A number of authorised guides operate year-round at Skaftafell (and at lesser-visited glacier tongues further east, towards Höfn). The largest companies, Icelandic Mountain Guides (p33) and **Glacier Guides** (Reykjavík 562 7000, Skaftafell 659 7000; www.glacierguides.is; 8.30am-6pm Apr-Oct, reduced hours Nov-Mar), have info and booking huts at Skaftafell, and you can talk to experts and get kitted out for glacier walks (warm clothes essential, waterproof gear and hiking boots available for hire).

Ice Caves

Winter visits to ice caves, glorious dimpled caverns of exquisite blue light, are accessible (usually at glacier edges) only from around November to March – they become unstable and unsafe in warmer weather. Temporary ice caves are created anew each season by the forces of nature, and are scouted by local experts. They must be visited with guides, who will ensure safety and correct equipment. As with glacier walks, tours generally involve getting kitted out (crampons, helmets etc), then driving to the glacier edge and taking a walk to reach the destination.

Local Guide (894 1317; www.localguide.is; Fagurhólsmýri; 9am-5pm) is the regional expert on ice caves in the Southeast. Other good, locally owned companies offering ice-cave exploration include **Glacier Adventure** (571 4577; www. glacieradventures.is), IceGuide (p42) and Glacier Trips (p42).

Fjallsárlón glacier lagoon (p40)

The Drive » About 15km east of Hólmur farm is a sign pointing the way north to Hoffell guesthouse.

---

⑬ Hoffellsjökull

En route to the **Hoffell Guesthouse** (Glacier World; ☑478 1514; www.glacierworld. is; d with/without bathroom kr30,500/20,500; 🛜), a signed, 4km gravel road leads to Hoffellsjökull glacier tongue, which calves into a small lake. There are some good short walks in the area, plus longer hikes.

At the guesthouse there are some excellent diversions open to all, including **quad-bike tours**. The most popular reason to stop by, though, is the chance to soak in a collection of geothermally heated **outdoor hot-pots** (kr600kr; ⌚7am-10pm).

The Drive » Head back to the Ring Road to drive the final 17km to Höfn. You'll need to take the turn-off south of the Ring Road, travelling on Rte 99 for the final 6km.

---

⑭ Höfn (p103)

Although it's no bigger than many European villages, the Southeast's main town feels like a sprawling metropolis after driving through the emptiness on either side. Its setting is stunning; on a clear day, wander down to the waterside, find a quiet bench and just gaze at Vatnajökull and its brotherhood of glaciers.

There are good areas for panorama-filled walks, including around the marshes and lagoons at the end of the promontory **Ósland** (about 1km beyond the harbour – head for the seamen's monument on the rise). The area is great for watching seabirds, though watch out for dive-bombing Arctic terns.

'Höfn' simply means 'harbour', and is pronounced like an unexpected hiccup (just say 'hup' while inhaling). The town relies heavily on fishing and fish processing, and is famous for its *humar* (langoustine). Come meal-time, the hottest tables are at innovative harbourside **Pakkhús** (☑478 2280; www.pakkhus. is; Krosseyjarvegur 3; mains kr3100-6790; ⌚noon-10pm mid-May–mid-Sep, 5-9pm mid-Sep–mid-May) and cute, chic **Humarhöfnin** (☑478 1200; www.humarhofnin.is; Hafnarbraut 4; mains kr2900-8400; ⌚noon-10pm Mar-Sep, to 9pm Oct-Nov).

East Iceland

3

As far as you can get from Reykjavík, Iceland's sparsely populated east doesn't announce itself as loudly as other parts of the country, preferring subtle charms over big-ticket attractions.

TRIP HIGHLIGHTS

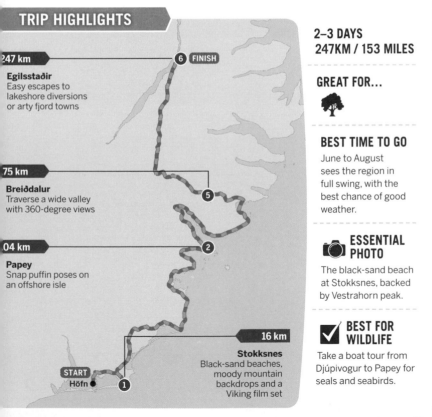

247 km

6 FINISH

Egilsstaðir
Easy escapes to lakeshore diversions or arty fjord towns

75 km

Breiðdalur
Traverse a wide valley with 360-degree views

5

104 km

2

Papey
Snap puffin poses on an offshore isle

16 km

Stokksnes
Black-sand beaches, moody mountain backdrops and a Viking film set

START
Höfn

1

2–3 DAYS
247KM / 153 MILES

GREAT FOR...

BEST TIME TO GO

June to August sees the region in full swing, with the best chance of good weather.

ESSENTIAL PHOTO

The black-sand beach at Stokksnes, backed by Vestrahorn peak.

BEST FOR WILDLIFE

Take a boat tour from Djúpivogur to Papey for seals and seabirds.

Stokksnes cape with a view of Vestrahorn mountain (p46)

45

3 East Iceland

Most travellers hit the accelerator and follow the over-eager Ring Road as it ploughs through the east, but they're missing some gems. This is a region that rewards slow travel: prepare yourself for superb vistas as the road skirts mountain peaks, steep-sided fjords, black-sand beaches and broad valleys. Stop to admire tiny fishing villages and take a boat trip to an island festooned with puffins.

TRIP HIGHLIGHT

➊ Stokksnes

From Höfn, rejoin the Ring Road (Rte 1) heading east, and after about 7km, just before the Ring Road enters a tunnel through the Almannaskarð pass, take the signposted road south to Stokksnes cape. After 4.5km, in a wild setting under moodily Gothic **Vestrahorn** mountain, you'll find a cool little outpost: the **Viking Cafe** (www.vikingcafe.is; waffles & cake kr900; ☺9am-7pm May-

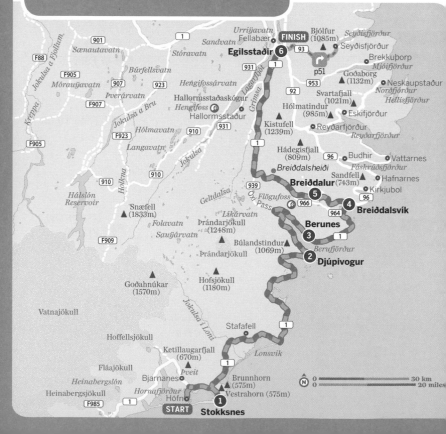

Oct), where coffee, waffles and cake are served.

The farm-owner runs the cafe, and he charges visitors a small fee (kr800) to explore his incredible property, including a photogenic Viking village film set and miles of black-sand beaches, where seals laze and the backdrop of Vestrahorn creates superb photos.

Note that the film set (built in 2009 by Icelandic film director Baltasar Kormakúr) may finally see action soon, when Baltasar directs *Vikings*, a long-gestating film project he started writing more than a decade ago. The set will hopefully remain in place after its film duties are done.

The Drive » Rejoin the Ring Road and head north. The 104km stretch around Iceland's southeast corner, between Höfn and Djúpivogur, is a scenic stretch, the road curving past only a handful of farms backed by precipitous peaks, and a swan-filled lagoon at Hvalnes Nature Reserve, where you can stop and stretch your legs. Note: no fuel stops, no toilets.

- - - - - - - - - - - -

TRIP HIGHLIGHT

② Djúpivogur (p104)

Djúpivogur's neat historic buildings, artists' workshops and small harbour are worth a look, but the main reason to visit this friendly fishing village is to catch the boat to **Papey**, a

---

PAPEY

The name of offshore island Papey (Friars' Island) suggests it was once a hermitage for the Irish monks who may have briefly inhabited Iceland before fleeing upon the arrival of the Norse. This small (2 sq km) and tranquil island was once a farm, but it's now uninhabited. As well as the local wildlife (puffins can be easily spotted from mid-April to early/mid-August), other highlights include the rock **Kastali** (the Castle), home to the 'hidden people'; a **lighthouse** built in 1922; and Iceland's oldest and smallest wooden **church** (from 1807).

---

small offshore island inhabited only by sunbathing seals and nesting seabirds, including a puffin posse. **Papeyjarferðir** (☎862 4399, 478 8119; www. djupivogur.is/papey; adult/ child kr10,000/5000) runs four-hour tours to the island, spotting wildlife en route and walking the island trails. Weather permitting, the boat departs Djúpivogur harbour at 1pm daily June to August.

Djúpivogur is actually one of the oldest ports in the country – it's been around since the 16th century, when German merchants brought goods to trade. These days the town has embraced the Cittaslow movement ('Slow Cities'), an offshoot of the Slow Food initiative, and there's a low-key, creative vibe and some al fresco art worth checking out, including *Eggin í Gleðivík*: 34 oversized eggs along the jetty, each one representing a local

bird. The large old fish factory (Bræðsla) hosts contemporary art exhibitions in summer.

The Drive » The Ring Road meanders around Berufjörður, a long, steep-sided fjord. The southwestern shore is dominated by the pyramid-shaped mountain Búlandstindur, rising 1069m above the water. There's also a nature reserve, Teigarhorn, renowned for zeolite crystals and home to some short walks. Note: there's an 8km stretch of gravel road near the head of Berufjörður.

- - - - - - - - - - - -

③ Berunes

Looking to break your journey somewhere remote and scenic? **Berunes HI Hostel** (☎869 7227, 478 8988; www.berunes. is; dm/d without bathroom kr5300/13,500, cottages from kr22,500; ☺Apr-Oct; @) ✿ is on a century-old farm run by affable Ólafur and his family. There are rooms in a wonderfully creaky old farmhouse plus newer buildings, and also a campsite and cottages. There's a summer evening restaurant, too.

On the farm next to Berunes is **Havarí** (📞663 5520; www.havari.is; Karlsstaðir; meals kr1200-1800; 🕐11am-9pm; 🅿 ♿), a warm, creative place owned by a young family that includes acclaimed musician Prins Póló. A converted barn is now a cafe and music venue – look out for events on the Facebook page, or stop by to try the tasty farm-made *bulsur* (vegan sausages). You can also order coffee, soup and waffles, and buy *sveitasnakk* (chips made from turnips). Also here: a cosy four-bedroom farmhouse for rent. Winter hours for Havarí are less concrete – call, or check Facebook.

The Drive » Follow the road as it skirts around Ósfjall mountain and runs along the impressive black-sand beach of Meleyri. The view west of here takes in Breiðdalur ('Broad Valley'), where the Ring Road continues. Take a signed right turn to reach Breiðdalsvík.

- - - - - - - - - - - -

❹ Breiðdalsvík (p104)

The tiny fishing village of Breiðdalsvík is beautifully positioned at the end of Breiðdalur. It's a quiet place – more a base for walking in the nearby hills and fishing the rivers and lakes than

Coastline at Djúpivogur (p47)

an attraction in itself. Stop by **Kaupfjélagið** (Sólvellir 23; light meals kr400-1650; ☺10am-7pm), the general store, for coffee and a bite. Its best features are the fun displays of vintage general-store items (some for sale) that were discovered in the attic during recent renovations.

Based in Breiðdalsvík, **Travel East** (☑471 3060; www.traveleast.is) is an agency that can arrange local tours and activities, from fishing to cycling and guided hiking. Boat cruises are popular – these leave a couple of times daily from May to September, and puffins and other seabirds are regularly sighted. Jeep tours can also be arranged, heading into the nearby mountains.

The Drive ›› From Breiðdalsvík you need to determine your preferred route to Egilsstaðir: west over a mountain road (Rte 1; 84km), or east along the fjord-side route (Rtes 92 and 96; 92km).

- - - - - - - - - - - - -

TRIP HIGHLIGHT

❺ Breiðdalur (p104)

The Ring Road travels west through the scenic Breiðdalur valley, nestled beneath colourful rhyolite peaks and cut by a popular fishing river, the Breiðdalsá. Take the turn-off to **Flögufoss**, a 60m-high waterfall (19km west of Breiðdalsvík), if you feel like a short walk.

The Drive ›› The road ascends steeply over Breiðdalsheiði

LOCAL EXPERIENCES

With its small population (around 11,000), distance from the capital, and with the Ring Road steaming quickly through it, East Iceland has struggled to get the traveller attention it deserves. **Tanni Travel** (☑476 1399; www.meetthelocals.is) hopes to change that, and is working with locals to create unique experiences. The agency is based in Eskifjörður but works all over the east, and offers a roster of guided village walks (daily from June to mid-September); it can also devise itineraries and connect you with guides and activities (particularly useful in winter). Unique in Iceland, it also offers travellers the chance to spend an evening dining in the home of locals (kr14,500 per person).

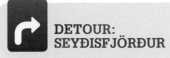

DETOUR: SEYÐISFJÖRÐUR

Start: ❻ Egilsstaðir (p51)

The Ring Road tracks inland for a large part of its journey through Iceland's east, meaning travellers often miss out on the treasures of the Eastfjords. This is one of Iceland's most spectacular regions, so a detour is warranted.

If you visit only one town in the Eastfjords, Seyðisfjörður should be it. Made up of multicoloured wooden houses and surrounded by snow-capped mountains and cascading waterfalls, obscenely picturesque Seyðisfjörður is the most historically and architecturally interesting town in East Iceland. It's also a friendly place with an international community of artists, musicians, craftspeople and students. There are fun hiking trails and activity options, great places to stay and superb eating options – try the super-fresh sushi at **Norð Austur Sushi & Bar** (☑787 4000; 2nd fl, Norðurgata 2; mains kr1890-4290; ☺6-10pm Sun-Thu, to 11pm Fri & Sat mid-May–mid-Sep) or pizzas at **Skaftfell** (☑472 1633; http://skaftfell.is/en/bistro; Austurvegur 42; mains kr1300-3500; ☺8am-10pm; ☎🅿🚹), a fabulous bistro-bar-cultural-centre. **Seyðisfjörður Tours** (☑785 4737; www.facebook.com/seydisfjordurtours; Norðurgata 6; ☺Jun-Aug, plus Sep by request) can rent you mountain bikes, take you on a guided walk or set you up on a scenic boat tour with a local fishing expert.

If the weather's good, the 27km drive from Egilsstaðir (take Rte 93, signed off Rte 1) is an absolute stunner, climbing to a high pass then descending along the waterfall-filled river Fjarðará.

Summer is the liveliest time to visit – but note that Wednesday nights are super-busy, as the ferry to Europe sails on Thursday mornings and rooms, meals and campsites in town are in hot demand. If you are taking the ferry, book your accommodation well ahead.

heath (note: gravel surface and hairpin turns, plus great views east over the valley to the coast) before continuing north to Egilsstaðir. Watch for Lagarfljót lake to come into view on your left.

TRIP HIGHLIGHT

❻ Egilsstaðir (p104)

The town of Egilsstaðir isn't exactly a ravishing beauty. It's the main regional transport hub, and a centre for local commerce, so its services are quite good (including quality accommodation and dining options). It's growing fast, but in a hotchpotch fashion.

Egilsstaðir's saving grace is its proximity to **Lagarfljót**, Iceland's third-largest lake. Since Saga times, tales have been told of a monster living in its depths. Whether you see a monster or not, the lake is a lovely stretch of water to circumnavigate by car. Rte 931, a mixture of sealed surfaces and gravel (gravel on the less-trafficked western shore), turns off the Ring Road about 10km south of Egilsstaðir and runs around the lake to Fellabær – a circuit of around 70km. Along the way are great diversions including forests, lakeside picnic areas, the museum **Skriðuklaustur** (☑471 2990; www.skriduklaustur.is; adult/child kr1000/free; ☺10am-6pm Jun-Aug, noon-5pm May & Sep) and its superb **cafe** (lunch buffet adult/child kr2990/1495; ☺10am-6pm Jun-Aug, noon-5pm May & Sep; 🚹) – go for the cake buffet, and spectacular **Hengifoss** waterfall.

North Iceland

4

Iceland's magnificent north is a geologist's dream. A wonderland of moonlike lava fields, belching mudpots, epic waterfalls, snowcapped peaks and whale-filled bays – this is Iceland at its best.

TRIP HIGHLIGHTS

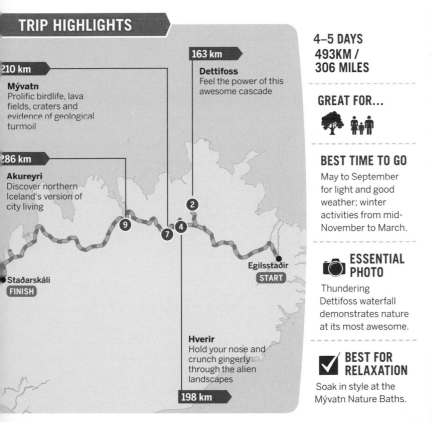

163 km

Dettifoss
Feel the power of this awesome cascade

210 km

Mývatn
Prolific birdlife, lava fields, craters and evidence of geological turmoil

286 km

Akureyri
Discover northern Iceland's version of city living

Staðarskáli
FINISH

Egilsstaðir
START

Hverir
Hold your nose and crunch gingerly through the alien landscapes

198 km

4–5 DAYS
493KM /
306 MILES

GREAT FOR...

BEST TIME TO GO
May to September for light and good weather; winter activities from mid-November to March.

ESSENTIAL PHOTO
Thundering Dettifoss waterfall demonstrates nature at its most awesome.

BEST FOR RELAXATION
Soak in style at the Mývatn Nature Baths.

Dettifoss (p55)

4 North Iceland

The region's top sights are variations on one theme: a grumbling, volcanically active earth. Nature's masterpieces are everywhere you look, and there are endless treats to uncover. Take in little Akureyri, with its surprising moments of big-city living; windy pastures full of stout Viking horses; white-water rapids ready to deliver an adrenaline kick; unhyped and underpopulated ski fields; and lonely peninsulas stretching out towards the Arctic Circle.

❶ Möðrudalur (p106)

Leaving Egilsstaðir the Ring Road (Rte 1) tracks north, then turns southwest to follow the Jökulsá á Dal river for about 30km. From here, the Ring Road cuts a path inland across the stark highlands of the northeast. The barren, grey-toned landscape is dotted with low hills and small lakes caused by melting snowfields.

This area has always been a difficult place

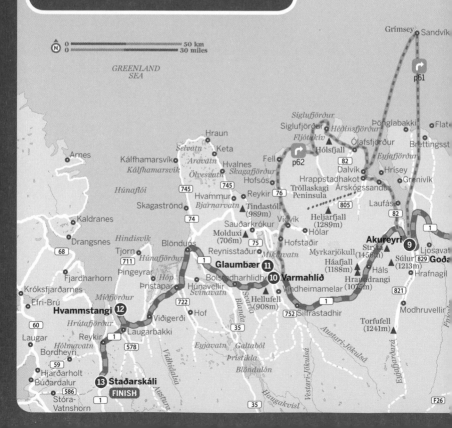

to eke out a living, and farms here are few and far between. Isolated Möðrudalur, an oasis in the desert, is the highest farm in Iceland at 469m. It's 8km south of the Ring Road on Rte 901, with the turn-off 104km west of Egilsstaðir. At Möðrudalur you'll find a popular mini-village, bustling in summer. **Fjalladýrð** (☎4711858; www.fjalladyrd.is; Möðrudalur; sites per person kr1350, d with/without bathroom kr35,000/15,900) is the name of the tourist service, with camping, accommodation and jeep

tours. Folks simply passing through Möðrudalur should stop for coffee and *kleina* (a traditional twisted doughnut), or try the farm-to-table dishes at **Fjallakaffi** (mains kr2290-7490; ⊙7am-10pm May-Sep, 9am-5pm Oct-Apr), the excellent restaurant here.

The Drive » Rejoin the Ring Road and press west through empty landscapes. After 26km you'll cross the bridge over the glacial river Jökulsá á Fjöllum, and 3km further is the sign indicating the 4WD-only Rte F88 to Askja in the highlands. Press on another 6km and you'll reach the sealed road

(Rte 862) to Dettifoss – take it, and drive 24km.

- - - - - - - - - - - - -

TRIP HIGHLIGHT

❷ Dettifoss

The power of nature can be seen in all its glory at Dettifoss, one of Iceland's most impressive waterfalls. The falls can be seen from either side of the canyon – Rte 862 links the Ring Road with the western bank of the falls, ending in a large car park and toilet facilities. From the car park, a 2.5km loop walk takes in the dramatic,

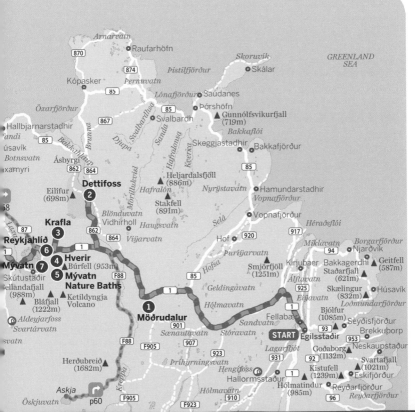

canyon-edge viewpoint of Dettifoss, plus views of a smaller cataract, **Selfoss**.

Although Dettifoss is only 45m high and 100m wide, a massive 400 cu metres of water thunders over its edge every second in summer, creating a plume of spray that can be seen 1km away. With the greatest volume of any waterfall in Europe, this truly is nature at its most spectacular. On sunny days, brilliant double rainbows form above the churning milky-grey glacial waters, and you'll have to jostle with the other visitors for the best views. Take care on the paths, made wet and slippery from the spray.

The Drive » Waterfall cravings sated, head south to rejoin the Ring Road, then head 20km west and take Rte 863 to reach Krafla, 7km north.

- - - - - - - - - - - -

❸ Krafla

Steaming vents and craters await at Krafla, an active volcanic region. Technically, Krafla is just an 818m-high mountain, but the name is now used for the entire area as well as a **geothermal power station** and the series of eruptions that created Iceland's most awesome lava field. There's a **visitor centre** (⏱10am-5pm Jun-Aug) at the power station if you're interested in learning about its workings. Beyond it is a great viewpoint over the landscapes.

Krafla's most impressive attraction is the **Leirhnjúkur** crater and its solfataras. In 1975, the Krafla Fires began with a small lava eruption by Leirhnjúkur, and after nine years of on-and-off action Leirhnjúkur became the ominous-looking, sulphur-encrusted mud hole that tourists love today. The earth's crust here is extremely thin and in places the ground is ferociously hot. A well-defined track leads northwest to Leirhnjúkur from the parking area; with all the volcanic activity, high temperatures, bubbling mudpots and steaming vents, it's best not to stray from the marked paths.

The Drive » Once you're back on the Ring Road, it's barely a few metres to reach the next turn. Let the steam and the stench guide you.

- - - - - - - - - - - -

TRIP HIGHLIGHT

❹ Hverir

The magical, ochre-toned world of Hverir (also called Hverarönd) is a lunarlike landscape of mud cauldrons, steaming vents, radiant mineral deposits and piping fumaroles. Belching mudpots and the powerful stench of sulphur may not sound enticing, but Hverir's ethereal allure grips every passer-by.

Safe pathways through the features have been roped off; to avoid risk of serious injury and damage to the natural

---

WINTER WONDERS

You're probably aware that the number of visitors to Iceland has skyrocketed in recent years. You may well be asking: what if there was a way to experience Iceland's awesome outdoors, but with smaller crowds? There is: visit in winter. For the Northern Lights, yes, but so much more.

Akureyri, the Tröllaskagi Peninsula and Mývatn are all winter wonderlands. Akureyri has winter festivals and easy access to Iceland's biggest ski field at Hlíðarfjall (p110). The Tröllaskagi Peninsula offers smaller ski fields plus great heliskiing (peak months: March and April). Mývatn has activities such as snowshoe and cross-country ski tours, snowmobiling on the frozen lake and dog sledding in the hills.

Packages can be arranged that cover a variety of activities plus transfers and accommodation. A good tip is to travel from around February, when daylight hours are increasing.

Volcanic crater pool at Krafla

features avoid any lighter-coloured soil and respect the ropes.

A walking trail loops from Hverir up **Námafjall ridge** behind the site. This 30-minute climb provides a grand vista over the steamy surroundings.

The Drive » The Ring Road climbs the pinky-orange Námafjall ridge that backs Hverir, and tumbles down its far side towards Mývatn. Pull over at the viewpoint on your left for impressive lake views. You'll pass Bjarnarflag, an active geothermal area. Turn left at the turquoise pond (actually a toxic remnant of a diatomite plant).

❺ Mývatn Nature Baths

Northern Iceland's answer to the Blue Lagoon, **Mývatn Nature Baths** (Jarðböðin; 📞464 4411; www.myvatnnaturebaths. is; adult/child kr4000/free; ⏲9am-midnight Jun-Aug, noon-10pm Sep-May) is 3km east of Reykjahlíð and the Mývatn lakeshore. Although it's smaller than its sparkling, magnetic southern counterpart, it's also cheaper and less hyped (probably a good thing), and it's a gorgeous place to soak in the powder blue, mineral-rich waters and enjoy the panorama. After a relaxing soak, try one of the two natural steam baths and/or a meal at the on-site cafeteria.

The Drive » You'll barely get comfortable before you reach the next stop, 3km west of the Nature Baths.

❻ Reykjahlíð (p106)

On the northeastern lakeshore, Reykjahlíð is Mývatn region's main village and obvious base. There's little to it beyond a collection of guesthouses and hotels, a supermarket, a petrol station and an information

ANDREW MAYOVSKYY/SHUTTERSTOCK ©

centre. Accommodation here (and everywhere in the Mývatn area) is in strong demand, and the prices reflect this. Book well ahead.

The well-informed **Mývatnsstofa Visitor Centre** (☎464 4390; www.visitmyvatn.is; Hraunvegur 8, Reykjahlíð; ☺7.30am-6pm Jun-Aug, shorter hours Sep-May), by the supermarket, has good displays on the local geology, and can book tours and transport. Pick up a copy of the useful *Mývatn* brochure, which gives an excellent overview of hiking trails in the area. All tours and buses leave from the car park here.

The Drive ⟩⟩ Mývatn lake is encircled by a 36km sealed road (Rte 1 on the western and northern shores, and Rte 848 on the southern and eastern shoreline). Most sleeping and eating options are in Reykjahlíð or at Vógar, a hamlet about 2.5km south of Reykjahlíð. A further cluster of options lie along the southern lakeshore at Skútustaðir.

- - - - - - - - - -

TRIP HIGHLIGHT

7 Mývatn (p106)

Travelling clockwise around the lake from Reykjahlíð, geological wonders are thick on the ground, with the eastern shoreline holding the most appeal. The classic tephra ring **Hverfjall** (also called Hverfell) is an ancient and near-symmetrical crater, rising 452m across and stretching 1040m across. It's an awe-inspiring landmark in Mývatn, and it's a relatively easy walk up to the top from a parking area at the ring's northwest.

Next is the giant jagged lava field at **Dimmuborgir** (literally 'Dark Castles'). A series of nontaxing, colour-

---

DETOUR: HÚSAVIK

Start: 6 Reykjahlíð (p57)

Húsavík, Iceland's whale-watching capital, has become a firm favourite on travellers' itineraries – and with its colourful houses, unique museums and stunning snowcapped peaks across Skjálfandi bay, it's easily the northeast's prettiest fishing town. It's 55km from Reykjahlíð via Rte 87. You can take a different route back to the Ring Road if you wish – take Rte 85 and you'll rejoin the road just a kilometre or two west of Goðafoss waterfall.

Although there are other Iceland locales where you can do whale-watching tours (Reykjavík and Akureyri, for example), Húsavík has become Iceland's premier whale-watching destination, with up to 11 species coming here to feed in summer. The best time to see whales is between June and August. This is, of course, the height of tourist season, but you'll have a near-100% chance of seeing cetaceans.

Four whale-watching companies now operate from Húsavík harbour. Don't stress too much about picking an operator; prices are similar and services are comparable for the standard three-hour tour (guiding and warm overalls supplied, plus hot drinks and a pastry). Where the differences are clear, however, is in the excursions that go beyond the standard. When puffins are nesting (from roughly mid-April to mid-August), all companies offer tours that incorporate whale watching with a sail by the puffin-festooned island of Lundey – **North Sailing** (☎464 7272; www.northsailing.is; Garðarsbraut; 3hr tour adult/child kr10,500/4200) does this on board an atmospheric old schooner over four hours (hoisting sails when conditions are right), while **Gentle Giants** (☎464 1500; www.gentlegiants.is; Garðarsbraut; 3hr tour adult/child kr10,300/4200) does it over 2½ hours in a high-speed rigid inflatable boat.

coded walking trails runs through the easily anthropomorphised landscape. There's a good cafe here, too.

The forested lava headland at **Höfði** is one of the area's gentlest landscapes. Wildflowers, birch and spruce trees cover the bluffs, while the tiny islands and crystal-clear waters attract migratory birds. From footpaths along the shore you'll see small caves and stunning *klasar* (lava pillars).

The south side of the lake lures with its epic cache of pseudocraters. The **Skútustaðagígar** pseudocraters were formed when molten lava flowed into the lake, triggering a series of gas explosions. These dramatic green dimples then came into being when trapped subsurface water boiled and popped, forming small scoria cones and craters.

Western Mývatn offers some of the best **birdwatching** in Iceland, with more than 115 species recorded in the area – including 28 species of ducks. For some birdwatching background, swing by the excellent **Sigurgeir's Bird Museum** (Fuglasafn Sigurgeirs; 464 4477; www.fuglasafn.is; adult/child kr1200/600; 9am-6pm Jun-Aug, reduced hours Sep-May).

The Drive » The Ring Road continues west from the lake

THE LOWDOWN ON MÝVATN

Mývatn (pronounced *mee*-vaht) is the calm, shallow lake at the heart of a volatile volcanic area that sits squarely on the Mid-Atlantic Ridge. Nature's violent masterpieces are everywhere: crazy-coloured mudpots, huge craters and jagged lava fields. Once you've had your fill of geology gone wild, mellow out with walks, bicycle rides and top-notch birdwatching (geese, golden plovers, swans and ducks) – and plenty of soaks at the Nature Baths.

Most of the points of interest are linked by the lake's looping road. The area (plus the awesome natural highlights east of Reykjahlíð at Hverir and Krafla) can be explored in a full and busy day, but two days is better, and if you want to hike and explore more distant mountains and lava fields (or take a day tour to Askja in the highlands), allow at least three days.

The downside to Mývatn (whose name translates as 'Midge Lake') are the dense midge clouds that appear during summer, with tiny insects intent on flying up your nose. You may want to wear a head net (which you can buy at the supermarket in Reykjahlíð, and elsewhere) – and pray for a good wind, which seems to curtail their activity.

region. About 33km from Mývatn's southwest corner toward Akureyri you'll happen across heavenly, horseshoe-shaped Goðafoss.

— — — — — — — — — —

❽ Goðafoss

Goðafoss (Waterfall of the Gods) rips straight through the Bárðardalur lava field along the Ring Road, and it's a magnet that pulls most drivers off the road for a closer look. Although smaller and less powerful than some of Iceland's other chutes, it's definitely one of the most beautiful. There are two car parks – one on the Ring Road, the other down the road

beside the petrol station. Take the path behind the falls for a less-crowded viewpoint.

The falls play an important part in Icelandic history. At the Alþingi (National Assembly) in the year 1000, the *lögsögumaður* (law speaker), Þorgeir, was forced to make a decision on Iceland's religion. After 24 hours of meditation, he declared the country a Christian nation. On his way home he passed the waterfall near his farm, and tossed in his pagan carvings of the Norse gods, thus bestowing the falls' present name.

DETOUR: ASKJA & THE HIGHLANDS

Start: ⑥ Reykjahlíð (p57)

Iceland's highlands are so barren and remote that astronauts held astrogeological training exercises here before the 1969 lunar landings. The highlands are true wilderness, with practically no services, accommodation or bridges (driving here involves fording rivers, and large 4WD vehicles are essential). Road access is only open a few months a year; the easiest way to visit is on a tour.

A number of operators run super-Jeep tours to Askja and surrounds, from mid-June (when the roads open) until as late into September as weather permits. Day tours take around 12 hours and leave from Reykjahlíð. Recommended operators include **Saga Travel** (☎558 8888; www.sagatravel.is) and **Geo Travel** (☎864 7080; www.geotravel.is). Another operator, **Fjalladýrð** (☎471 1858; www.fjalladyrd.is), runs from Möðrudalur.

The usual access road is Rte F88, which leaves the Ring Road 32km east of Mývatn; the road is known as the Askja Route (Öskjuleið).

For much of the way the F88 is a flat journey, following the western bank of the **Jökulsá á Fjöllum** glacier river, meandering across tephra wasteland and winding circuitously through rough, tyre-abusing sections of the 4400-sq-km **Ódáðahraun** (Evil Deeds Lava Field).

After a long journey through the lava- and flood-battered plains, things perk up at the lovely oasis of **Herðubreiðarlindir**, at the foot of **Herðubreið** (1682m), the Icelanders' beloved 'Queen of the Mountains'. The route then wanders westward through dunes and lava flows to a parking area, where you leave your vehicle to walk the remaining 2.5km to the immense, 50-sq-km caldera.

Askja was created by a colossal explosion of tephra in 1875. Part of the collapsed magma chamber contains sapphire-blue lake **Öskjuvatn**, the second-deepest in Iceland at 220m. Near the northeast corner is **Víti**, a tepid pool in a crater where the milky-blue water (around 25°C) is popular for a swim and soak, although access generally involves a bit of a scramble.

The Drive » It's a scenic drive west to Eyjafjörður and Akureyri. Note that a 7.5km-long road tunnel is being built on Eyjafjörður's eastern side, which will shorten the Ring Road journey by about 16km. Once it opens (likely sometime in 2017), drivers will be able to avoid the mountain pass Víkurskarð, which is often blocked by winter snows.

- - - - - - - - - - - -

TRIP HIGHLIGHT

⑨ Akureyri (p109)

Akureyri stands strong as Iceland's second city, but a Melbourne, Manchester or Montreal it is not. And how could it be? There are only 18,000 residents! Despite its diminutive size, you can expect cool cafes, quality restaurants and something of a late-night bustle – a far cry from other towns in rural Iceland. With its scenic setting, relaxed attitude and extensive accommodation choices, it's a natural base for exploring the north.

Akureyri nestles at the head of Eyjafjörður, Iceland's longest (60km) fjord, at the base of snowcapped peaks. In summer, well-tended gardens belie the location, just a stone's throw from the Arctic Circle. Lively winter festivals and some of Iceland's best skiing provide plenty of off-peak (and off-piste) appeal. It's a place geared for small pleasures and gentle strolling. Stop at the botanic gardens, **Lystigarðurinn** (www.lystigardur.akureyri.is; Eyrarlandsholt; ⊙8am-10pm Mon-Fri, 9am-10pm Sat & Sun Jun-Sep) **FREE**, and admire **Akureyrarkirkja** (www.akureyrarkirkja.is; Eyrarlandsvegur; ⊙10am-4pm Mon-Fri), the landmark church designed by the same architect responsible for Reykjavík's Hallgrímskirkja. Take it easy at the local swimming pool **Sundlaug Akureyrar** (Þingvallastræti 21; adult/child kr750/200; ⊙6.45am-9pm Mon-Fri, 8am-7.30pm Sat & Sun; 👶), and indulge in some dining, drinking and shopping along Hafnarstræti. If there's a live show at **Græni Hatturinn** (http://graenihatturinn.is; Hafnarstræti 96), snap up a ticket – this intimate venue is the best place in town to see live music (and one of the best in the country).

There are also plenty of ways to get out among the surrounding landscapes – from horse rides to hikes, whale-watching cruises to golf under the midnight sun. Visit www.visitakureyri.is for more info, and consider joining a tour with the likes of **Saga Travel** (📞558 8888; www.sagatravel.is).

The Drive » The highlight of the 93km Ring Road stretch between Akureyri and Varmahlíð is Öxnadalur, a narrow, 30km-long valley. Stunning peaks and thin pinnacles of rock flank the mountain pass.

---

⑩ Varmahlíð (p113)

This Ring Road service centre is slightly more than a road junction and yet not quite a town, and it's a great base for white-water rafting and horse riding. Most activity operators have a base along the sealed Rte 752, just west of the township's large N1 petrol station complex.

The northwest region is horse country, and companies in and around Varmahlíð offer menus of shorter rides (one to two hours) for beginners, plus longer day outings in wild landscapes. A few companies run week-long expeditions into the highlands. **Hestasport** (📞453 8383; www.riding.is; Rte 752) is one of Iceland's most respected riding outfits, and runs a smart

DETOUR: GRÍMSEY

Start: ⑨ Akureyri (p60)

Best known as Iceland's only true piece of the Arctic Circle, the remote island of Grímsey, 40km from the mainland, is a lonely little place where birds outnumber people by about 10,000 to one. The island is small (5 sq km, with a year-round population of 60), but the welcome is big.

Grímsey's appeal probably lies less in the destination itself, and more in what it represents. Tourists flock here to snap up their 'I visited the Arctic Circle' certificate and pose for a photo with the 'You're standing on the Arctic Circle' monument (the location of the actual line moves a little each year due to axial tilt). Afterwards, there's plenty of time to appreciate the windswept setting. Scenic coastal cliffs and dramatic basalt formations make a popular home for dozens of species of seabirds, including loads of puffins, plus the kamikaze Arctic tern.

If sleeping inside the Arctic Circle sounds too good to pass up, two small guesthouses offer accommodation.

There are a number of options for reaching Grímsey. Year-round, there are flight and ferry connections a few times a week. Flights depart from Akureyri; journey time is half an hour. Ferry services run from Dalvík, 43km north of Akureyri; sailing time is three hours one way. Air and boat excursions are an option in summer months, with Akureyri the hub for these. For more info, see www.akureyri.is/grimsey.

complex of cottages in town. The lovely farm **Lýtingsstaðir** (☑453 8064; www.lythorse.com; Rte 752; 1/2hr horse ride kr6000/7800) has a great program of short and long rides, plus accommodation.

Varmahlíð also gives access to northern Iceland's best white-water rafting. **Viking Rafting** (☑823 8300; www.vikingrafting.com; Rte 752)

leads trips on the high-octane Austari-Jökulsá (East Glacial River; Class 4+ rapids) and the more placid, family-friendly Vestari-Jökulsá (West Glacial River; Class 2+ rapids).

The Drive » Following Rte 75 north from Varmahlíð leads to the 18th-century turf-farm museum at Glaumbær. It's the best museum of its type in northern

Iceland and worth the easy 8km detour off the Ring Road.

----

⑪ Glaumbær

The traditional Icelandic turf farm was a complex of small separate buildings, connected by a central passageway. At the photogenic **Glaumbær** (www.glaumbaer.is; adult/child kr1500/free; ⏱9am-5pm May, 9am-6pm Jun–mid-Sep, 10am-4pm Mon-Fri mid-Sep–mid-Oct) museum you can see this style of construction, with some building compartments stuffed full of period furniture, equipment and utensils. It gives a fascinating insight into the cramped conditions of the era.

Also on the site are two 19th-century houses – one is home to **Áskaffi**, an impossibly quaint tearoom with old-world atmosphere and doll's-house dishware.

The Drive » Return to Varmahlíð and reconnect with the Ring Road, which tracks west then northwest through Langidalur (Long Valley) to the nondescript service town of Blönduós. From Blönduós, the road heads southwest through windswept landscapes and past fields of horses; take the turn-off at Rte 72, which leads 6km to the town of Hvammstangi.

----

⑫ Hvammstangi (p113)

Sweet, slow-paced Hvammstangi builds its appeal around the

⇨ DETOUR: TRÖLLASKAGI

Start: ⑨ Akureyri (p60)

Tröllaskagi (Troll Peninsula) rests its mountainous bulk between the scenic fjords of Skagafjörður and Eyjafjörður. Here, the craggy mountains, deep valleys and gushing rivers are more reminiscent of the Westfjords than the gentle hills that roll through most of northern Iceland. In great news for travellers seeking spectacular road trips, tunnels now link the northern Tröllaskagi townships of Siglufjörður and Ólafsfjörður, once dead-end towns that saw little tourist traffic.

The journey from Akureyri to Varmahlíð along the Ring Road (Rte 1) measures 95 very scenic kilometres, but if you have some time up your sleeve and a penchant for getting off the beaten track, the 186km journey between those two towns following the Tröllaskagi coastline (Rtes 82 and 76) conjures up some magical scenery, dramatic road tunnels, and plenty of excuses to pull over and explore. Worthy pit stops include ferries to offshore islands Grímsey and Hrísey, whale-watching tours on Eyjafjörður, a **microbrewery** (Kaldi Beer; ☑466 2505; www.bruggsmidjan.is; Öldugata 22, Árskógssandur; tour kr2000; ⏱tours by appointment 11am-3pm), ski fields, Siglufjörður's colourful harbourfront and outstanding **herring museum** (Síldarminjasafnið; www.sild.is; Snorragata 10; adult/child kr1500/free; ⏱10am-6pm Jun-Aug, 1-5pm May & Sep, by appointment Oct-Apr), and Hofsós' dreamy fjord-side **swimming pool** (Suðurbraut; adult/child kr700/300; ⏱9am-9pm Jun-Aug, 7am-1pm & 5-8pm Mon-Fri, 11am-3pm Sat & Sun Sep-May).

Hvammstangi

local seal colonies. Visitors come to take a seal-watching cruise, go horse riding in the area, or drive the scenic loop around the Vatnsnes Peninsula. The town's prime attraction is the **Icelandic Seal Centre** (☎451 2345; www.selasetur.is; adult/child kr950/free; ☉9am-7pm Jun-Aug, 9am-4pm May & Sep, noon-3pm Tue-Sat Apr & Oct) on the harbourfront, where you can learn about the history and conservation of the area's seals.

With time up your sleeve, consider taking a couple of hours to drive around the starkly beautiful **Vatnsnes Peninsula**.

It's about 82km in total, from the Ring Road to Hvammstangi and around the peninsula on Rte 711, a gravel road (drive slowly).

On Vatnsnes' west coast, stop by storied **Illugastaðir** farm. A 10-minute walk through bird-filled fields leads from the car park to a popular site for sun-baking seals. On the east coast, stop at the photogenic 15m-high sea stack called **Hvítserkur**, which looks like a huge stone beast drinking from the water. Nearby, a walking path takes you down to a scenic black-sand beach

and views to a large seal haul-out site.

The Drive » Rejoin the Ring Road; from Hvammstangi it's about 35km to the next stop.

- - - - - - - - - - - -

⑬ Staðarskáli

The inlet of little Hrútafjörður marks the divide between northwest Iceland and the West. As you follow the Ring Road, you'll encounter Staðarskáli. No more than a road junction with a big, busy N1 petrol station and cafeteria, Staðarskáli acts as a popular leg-stretching spot for motorists.

West Iceland

5

Diverse West Iceland offers everything from windswept beaches and historic villages to awe-inspiring volcanic and glacial terrain in one neat little package.

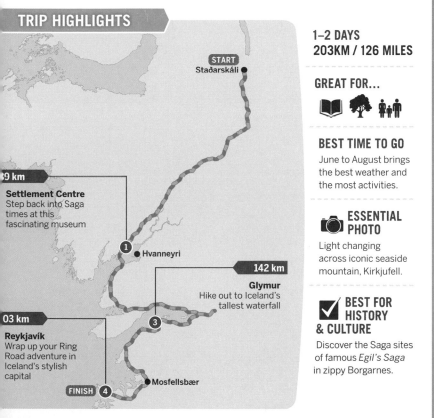

START
Staðarskáli

9 km

Settlement Centre
Step back into Saga times at this fascinating museum

1 Hvanneyri

142 km

Glymur
Hike out to Iceland's tallest waterfall

3

03 km

Reykjavík
Wrap up your Ring Road adventure in Iceland's stylish capital

FINISH 4   Mosfellsbær

1–2 DAYS
203KM / 126 MILES

GREAT FOR...

BEST TIME TO GO
June to August brings the best weather and the most activities.

ESSENTIAL PHOTO
Light changing across iconic seaside mountain, Kirkjufell.

BEST FOR HISTORY & CULTURE
Discover the Saga sites of famous *Egil's Saga* in zippy Borgarnes.

Kirkjufell (p68)

5 West Iceland

Geographically close to Reykjavík yet far, far away in sentiment, West Iceland (known as Vesturland) is a splendid blend of Iceland's offerings. Two of the best known sagas, *Egil's Saga* and *Laxdæla Saga,* took place along the region's brooding waters, marked today by haunting cairns and an exceptional museum in lively Borgarnes. The long arm of Snæfellsnes Peninsula, inland lava tubes and remote highland glaciers are added enticements.

TRIP HIGHLIGHT

❶ Borgarnes (p114)
Follow the Ring Road from Staðarskáli's petrol station 89km south to Borgarnes. You'll pass through rolling plains along the Norðurá river valley, with buttes rising in the distance; on clear days, you can see all the way to the ice cap at Langjökull. Around Hraunsnef you'll enter a rich lava-field zone with day hikes, and finally pass through light forest and summer house

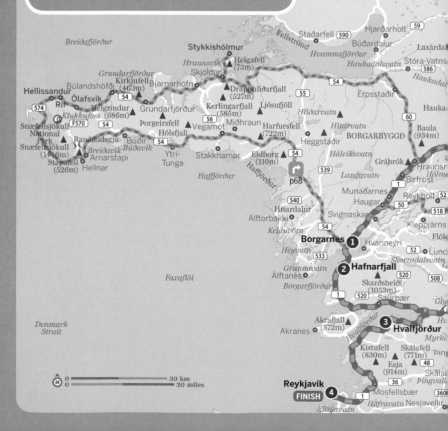

encampments around Munaðarnes, before descending into the river deltas and fjord zone around Borgarnes.

Buzzy Borgarnes, on a scenic promontory along the broad waters of **Borgarfjörður**, was the landing zone for several of Iceland's famous first settlers. Housed in an imaginatively restored warehouse by the harbour, the fascinating **Settlement Centre** (Land-námssetur Íslands; ✆437 1600; www.settlement centre.is; Brákarbraut 13-15; adult/child 1 exhibition kr1900/free, 2 exhibitions kr2500/free; ◷10am-9pm) offers insights into the history of Icelandic settlement and brings alive the story of one of its most famous settlers, poet-warrior Egill Skallagrímsson (the man behind *Egil's Saga*). The centre has also placed cairns throughout town marking key sites from *Egil's Saga*.

Borg á Mýrum (Rock in the Marshes; Rte 54) `FREE`, just northwest of Borgarnes on Rte 54, is where Skallagrímur Kveldúlfs-son, Egill's father, made his farm at Settlement. It was named for the large rock *(borg)* behind the farmstead. You can walk up to the **cairn** for super views. The small **cemetery** includes an ancient rune-inscribed gravestone. Ásmundur Sveinsson's **sculpture** represents Egill mourn-ing the death of his sons and his rejuvenation in poetry.

To unwind after your historical studies, visit Borgarnes' excellent fjord-side **geothermal pool** (www.borgarbyggd. is; Þorsteinsgata; adult/child kr600/250; ◷6am-10pm Mon-Fri, 9am-6pm Sat & Sun).

The Drive ≫ Zip a mere 3.5km south on the Ring Road crossing Borgarnes' long sweep of causeway to reach the trailhead for Hafnarfjall, the mountain rising precipitously from the water's edge south of the city.

❷ Hafnarfjall

The dramatically sheer mountain **Hafnarfjall** (844m) rises south across the fjord from Borgar-nes. You can climb it along a 7km path from the trailhead on Rte 1, near the southern base of the causeway into Borgarnes. Be careful of slippery scree cliffs once you ascend. If you make it all the way up the steep slopes, you'll get sweep-ing views from the top.

For the more domesti-cally inclined, find your way to off-the-beaten-path village Hvan-neyri, 12km northeast of Hafnarfjall, to visit **Ullarselið** (✆437 0077; www.ull.is; Hvanneyri; ◷11am-5pm Jun-Aug, 1-5pm Thu-Sat Sep-May), a fantastic wool centre that's part of the Agricultural Museum of Iceland. Handmade sweaters, scarves, hats and blankets share space with skeins of beautiful hand-spun yarn, and in-teresting bone and shell buttons. Plus there are needles and patterns to get you started. Look out for local Borgarfjörður designs featuring geese, ptarmigan or salmon.

Skemma Cafe (Skem-man Kaffihús; ✆868 8626; www.facebook.com/skemman cafe; Agricultural Museum of Iceland complex, Havnneyri; snacks 890-1350; ◷noon-5pm Jun–mid-Aug), in the same complex, in a renovated building from 1896,

67

has a sunny deck and a range of soups, cakes and coffees.

The Drive » This drive will skirt you around the base of Hafnarfjall and 28km along inland mountains, with glistening ocean just to the west. Turn east at Rte 47 to reach and follow Hvalfjörður's edge. Those in a hurry to reach Reykjavík can skip the fjord by continuing on the Ring Road straight through the 5.7km-long tunnel beneath the fjord.

TRIP HIGHLIGHT

❸ Hvalfjörður (p117)

This sparkling fjord is about 30km long, and lies between Akranes and Mosfellsbær. The lush area feels quite pastoral despite being a mere 30-minute drive from the capital. It is the site of a whaling station (*hvalur* means whale in Icelandic) and an aluminium smelting plant (not as unsightly as it sounds!). Interestingly, during WWII the fjord contained a submarine station; over 20,000 American and British soldiers passed through.

The **church** at the Saurbær farmstead contains beautiful stained-glass work by Gerður Helgadóttir. It's named Hallgrímskirkja (the same name as the famous church in Reykjavík) for Reverend Hallgrímur Pétursson, who served here from 1651 to 1669. He composed Iceland's most popular religious work, *Passion Hymns*.

Glymur, Iceland's highest waterfall at 198m (though some dispute that it's the highest, alleging that a taller one was found in 2010), lies at the head of Hvalfjörður. You can reach the trailhead by following the turn-off to Botnsdalur. From the end

DETOUR: SNÆFELLSNES PENINSULA

Start: ❶ Borgarnes (p66)

Sparkling fjords, dramatic volcanic peaks, sheer sea cliffs, sweeping golden beaches and crunchy lava flows make up the diverse and fascinating landscape of the 100km-long Snæfellsnes Peninsula. The area is crowned by the glistening ice cap Snæfellsjökull, immortalised in Jules Verne's *Journey to the Centre of the Earth*. It offers a cross-section of the best Iceland has to offer in a very compact region.

You'll circle the peninsula over the course of one long day, or two leisurely days, on Rte 54, starting at **Stykkishólmur**, on the populated northern coast. It is the region's largest town and super quaint to boot. Moving west along the northern coast, you'll pass smaller townships perfect for joining a whale- or puffin-viewing tour. Or head out to the windswept point at **Öndverðarnes** for lighthouses and occasional sightings of whales offshore. As you make this westerly drive, look for **Kirkjufell** near the town of **Grundarfjörður**; it's an iconic mountain that appears often on posters or in movies, and is backed by vibrant cascades.

On the western part of the peninsula, **Snæfellsjökull National Park** (☏ 436 6860; www.snaefellsjokull.is) encompasses not only its eponymous glacier, but bird sanctuaries, lava fields and other volcanic craters. You'll find the park **visitor centre** (☏ 436 6888, 591 2000; www.snaefellsjokull.is; Malarrif; ⏰10am-5pm Jun-Sep, to 4pm Mon-Fri Oct-May; 🛜) at the lighthouse at **Malarrif**; there are excellent online maps of the area as well. The quiet southern coast is lined with remote beaches and has several good horse farms along the verdant meadows that lie beneath towering inland crags. There is a scenic coastal walk between the hamlets of **Hellnar** and **Arnarstapi**.

Follow Rte 54 back inland and then south to where it joins the Ring Road just to the north of Borgarnes.

Reykjavík city centre

of the bumpy road, you must then hike a couple of hours on rough trails to reach the cascades. Note that a log is placed to bridge a river along the way only in summer.

On the southern side of Hvalfjörður you'll find dramatic mount **Esja** (914m), a great spot for wilderness hiking. The most popular trail to the summit begins at Esju-berg, just north of Mos-fellsbær, and ascends via Kerhólakambur (850m) and Kistufell (830m).

The Drive » From the southern shore of Hvalfjörður, rejoin the Ring Road and travel the 28km into Reykjavík. As you leave raw mountains and shining shores behind, you'll start to see the profile of Hallgrímskirkja rising up on Reykjavík's peninsula. To head into the centre, leave the Ring Road at Rte 49 and continue due west.

TRIP HIGHLIGHT

❹ Reykjavík (p74)

The world's most norther-ly capital combines colourful buildings, crea-tive people, eye-popping design, wild nightlife and a capricious soul to as-tonishing effect. In many ways Reykjavík is strik-ingly cosmopolitan for its size. After all, Reykjavík

GAIL JOHNSON/SHUTTERSTOCK ©

is merely a town by international standards, and yet it's loaded with excellent museums, captivating art, rich culinary choices, and offbeat cafes and bars. Add a backdrop of snow-topped mountains, churning seas and crystal-clear air, and you, like many visitors, may fall helplessly in love, returning home already saving to come back.

Start with a walk around the **Old Reykjavík** quarter near **Tjörnin** lake, then peruse the city's best museums, such as the impressive **National Museum** (Þjóðminjasafn Íslands; ☎530 2200; www. nationalmuseum.is; Suðurgata 41; adult/child kr1500/free; ⊙10am-5pm May–mid-Sep, closed Mon mid-Sep–Apr; 🚌1, 3, 6, 12, 14), **Reykjavík**

DETOUR: UPPER BORGARBYGGÐ

Start: ❶ Borgarnes (p66)

Inland from Borgarnes, up the river-twined valleys skirted by Rte 50 in the Upper Borgarbyggð area, you'll find fertile farms with deep history leading to powerful stone-strewn lava tubes and highlands, the gateway to ice caps beyond. The following route wends for some 130km and can be done in one long day; plan to overnight in Húsafell to include glacier or lava-tube activities.

Europe's biggest hot spring, **Deildartunguhver**, lies about 5km west of Reykholt, just off Rte 50. Look for billowing clouds of steam, which rise from scalding water bubbling from the ground (180L per second and 100°C!). A brand-new spa, **Krauma** (Deildartunguhver; ☎555 6066; www.krauma.is; Rte 50; adult/child kr4900/2900; ⊙10am-10pm), offers sleek hot pools, a cold pool and two steam rooms.

The interesting medieval study centre **Snorrastofa** (☎433 8000; www.snorrastofa. is; kr1200; ⊙10am-6pm May-Aug, to 5pm Mon-Fri Sep-Apr) in Reykholt is devoted to celebrated medieval poet, historian and statesman Snorri Sturluson, and is built on his old farm, where he was brutally slain.

Next, stop at **Hraunfossar** (Rte 518) – the name of this spectacular waterfall translates to Lava Field Waterfall because the crystalline water streams out from below the surrounding lava fields. Find the turnout on the north side of Rte 518, 6.5km west of Húsafell.

Tucked into an emerald, river-crossed valley, with the river Kaldá on one side and a dramatic lava field on the other, **Húsafell** is an encampment of summer cottages, and its chic **hotel** (☎435 1551; www.hotelhusafell.com; d incl breakfast from kr39,500; 🅿🛜) is a popular retreat for Reykjavikers.

The **Langjökull** ice cap is the second-largest glacier in Iceland, and the closest major glacier to Reykjavík. Do not attempt to drive up onto the glacier yourself. Tours depart from Húsafell (or Reykjavík): **Into the Glacier** (Langjökull Ice Cave; ☎578 2550; www.intotheglacier.is) ice cave is a major tourist attraction; **Mountaineers of Iceland** (☎580 9900; www.mountaineers.is) offers snowmobiling; and **Dog Sledding** (☎863 6733; www.dogsledding.is; tours from kr17,900) has summertime dog-sledding tours.

The largest lava tube in Iceland, 1100-year-old, 1.5km-long **Viðgelmir** (☎783 3600; www.thecave.is; tour per adult/child from kr6500/free) is located on private property near the farmstead Fljótstunga. It sparkles with ever-changing rock formations and has a stable walkway within it on which tours are conducted.

Old Harbour area in Reykjavík

Art Museum (Listasafn Reykjavíkur; www.artmuseum. is; adult/child kr1500/free) or the **Settlement Exhibition** (Landnámssýningin; 📞411 6370; www.reykjavikmuseum. is; Aðalstræti 16; adult/child kr1500/free; ☺9am-6pm). Wander up arty street **Skólavörðustígur** to the immense **Hallgrímskirkja** (📞510 1000; www.hallgrims kirkja.is; Skólavörðustígur; tower adult/child kr900/100; ☺9am-9pm Jun-Sep, to 5pm Oct-May). For a perfect view, take the elevator up the tower, then circle down to stroll **Laugavegur**, the main shopping drag.

Many of the more lively restaurants turn into party hang-outs at night. Eat well – the options seem endless these days and can fit any budget or palate – then enjoy people-watching and drinks as you join Reykjavík's notorious pub-crawl *djammið*.

After a late night out, get a big Icelandic brunch and visit **Harpa** (📞box office 528 5050; www.harpa.is; Austurbakki 2; ☺8am-midnight, box office 10am-6pm), the iconic concert hall, and then the **Old Harbour**. You can visit the harbour's museums, such as the **Víkin Maritime Museum** (Víkin Sjóminjasafnið; 📞517 9400; www.maritimemuseum. is; Grandagarður 8; adult/child kr1500/free; ☺10am-5pm; 🚌14), **Saga Museum** (📞511 1517; www.saga museum.is; Grandagarður 2; adult/child kr2100/800; ☺10am-6pm; 🚌14) or **Whales of Iceland** (📞571 0077; www.whalesoficeland. is; Fiskislóð 23-25; adult/child kr2900/1500; ☺10am-6pm Jun-Aug, to 5pm Sep-May; 🚌14), tour a chocolate factory at **Omnom Chocolate** (📞519 5959; www.omnomchocolate.com; Hólmaslóð 4, Grandi; adult/child kr3000/1500; ☺8am-5pm Mon-Fri), or head out on a **whale-watching tour**.

Destinations

Reykjavík (p74)

Iceland's addictive capital is where everything's at, and has a heady blend of fresh air, stylish design, artfully hip cafes and bars, fabulous and unusual museums plus a thriving restaurant scene.

The Golden Circle (p96)

In striking distance of the capital, this circuit comprises some standout natural attractions, including the world's oldest parliament, shifting tectonic plates, the original geyser and a stunning waterfall.

Akureyri (p109)

Iceland's second city packs a punch for a diminutive town and is worth getting to know. There's a quality restaurant and art scene, and the only decent nightlife beyond Reykjavík.

A vibrant small city with a lot of soul, Reykjavík is a cultural hub of innovative, offbeat art, music and design; its crisp clear air also thrums with culinary creativity and a rampant bar scene.

Reykjavík

History

Ingólfur Arnarson, a Norwegian fugitive, became the first official Icelander in AD 871, and Reykjavík was just a simple collection of farm buildings for centuries. It expanded in the 1700s when local sheriff Skúli Magnússon, the 'Father of Reykjavík', created factories to bypass a Danish monopoly. World War II was another boom period, and the city's architecture and cultural offerings have exploded once again with the recent rise in tourism to Iceland.

◉ Sights

The city centre contains most of Reykjavík's attractions, which range from interesting walking and shopping streets to excellent museums and lakeside or seaside promenades. Around the outskirts you find the places that Reykjavikers go to relax.

◉ Old Reykjavík

The area dubbed Old Reykjavík is the heart of the capital, and the focal point of many historic walking tours. The area is anchored by Tjörnin, the city-centre lake, and sitting between it and Austurvöllur park to the north are the Ráðhús (city hall) and Alþingi (parliament).

★**Settlement Exhibition** MUSEUM
(p71; Landnámssýningin; Map p82; ☑ 411 6370; www.reykjavikmuseum.is; Aðalstræti 16; adult/

child kr1500/free; ⊙ 9am-6pm) This fascinating archaeological ruin/museum is based around a 10th-century **Viking longhouse** unearthed here from 2001 to 2002, and the other settlement-era finds from central Reykjavík. It imaginatively combines technological wizardry and archaeology to give a glimpse into early Icelandic life. Don't miss the fragment of **boundary wall** at the back of the museum that is older still (and the oldest human-made structure in Reykjavík).

★**National Museum** MUSEUM
(p70; Þjóðminjasafn Íslands; Map p76; ☑ 530 2200; www.nationalmuseum.is; Suðurgata 41; adult/child kr1500/free; ⊙ 10am-5pm May–mid-Sep, closed Mon mid-Sep–Apr; ☐ 1, 3, 6, 12, 14) This superb museum displays artefacts from settlement to the modern age. Exhibits give an excellent overview of Iceland's history and culture, and the audio guide (kr300) adds loads of detail. The strongest section describes the Settlement Era – including how the chieftains ruled and the introduction of Christianity – and features swords, drinking horns, silver hoards and a powerful little **bronze figure of Thor**.

★**Reykjavík Art Museum – Hafnarhús** ART MUSEUM
(p71; Map p82; ☑ 411 6400; www.artmuseum. is; Tryggvagata 17; adult/child kr1500/free;

Tjörnin

⊙10am-5pm Fri-Wed, to 10pm Thu) Reykjavík Art Museum's Hafnarhús is a marvellously restored warehouse converted into a soaring steel-and-concrete exhibition space. Though the well-curated exhibitions of cutting-edge contemporary Icelandic art change frequently (think installations, videos, paintings and sculpture), you can always count on an area with the comic-book-style paintings of Erró (Guðmundur Guðmundsson), a political artist who has donated several thousand works to the museum.

★ Tjörnin LAKE
(p70; Map p82) This placid lake at the centre of the city is sometimes locally called the Pond. It echoes with the honks and squawks of over 40 species of visiting birds, including swans, geese and Arctic terns; feeding the ducks is a popular pastime for the under-fives. Pretty sculpture-dotted parks like Hljómskálagarður (Map p76) line the southern shores, and their paths are much used by cyclists and joggers. In winter hardy souls strap on ice skates and turn the lake into an outdoor rink.

⊙ Laugavegur & Skólavörðustígur

★ National Gallery of Iceland MUSEUM
(Listasafn Íslands; Map p82; ☑515 9600; www.listasafn.is; Fríkirkjuvegur 7; adult/child kr1500/free; ⊙10am-5pm mid-May–mid-Sep, 11am-5pm Tue-Sun mid-Sep–mid-May) This pretty stack of marble atriums and spacious galleries overlooking Tjörnin offers ever-changing exhibits drawn from the 10,000-piece collection. The museum can only exhibit a small sample at any time; shows range from 19th- and 20th-century paintings by Iceland's favourite sons and daughters (including Jóhannes Kjarval and Nína Sæmundsson) to sculptures by Sigurjón Ólafsson and others. The museum ticket also covers entry to the Ásgrímur Jónsson Collection (Map p82; ☑515 9625; www.listasafn.is; Bergstaðastræti 74; adult/child kr1000/free; ⊙2-5pm Tue, Thu & Sun mid-May–mid-Sep, 2-5pm Sun mid-Sep–Nov & Feb–mid-May) and Sigurjón Ólafsson Museum (p79).

★ Culture House ART MUSEUM
(Þjóðmenningarhúsið; Map p82; ☑530 2210; www.culturehouse.is; Hverfisgata 15; adult/child kr1200/free; ⊙10am-5pm May–mid-Sep, closed Mon mid-Sep–Apr) This fantastic collaboration between the National Museum, National Gallery and four other organisations creates a superbly curated exhibition covering the artistic and cultural heritage of Iceland from settlement to today. Priceless artefacts are arranged by theme, and highlights include 14th-century manuscripts, contemporary art and items including the skeleton of a great auk (now extinct). The renovated 1908 building is beautiful, with great views of the harbour, and a cafe on the ground floor. Check the website for free guided tours.

75

Reykjavík

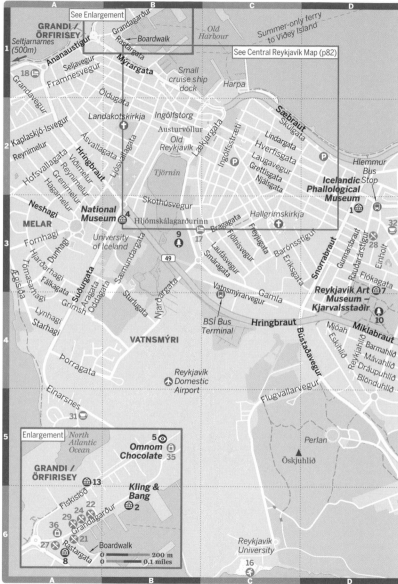

★ **Icelandic
Phallological Museum** MUSEUM
(Hið Íslenzka Reðasafn; Map p76; ☎561 6663;
www.phallus.is; Laugavegur 116; adult/child
kr1250/free; ☉10am-6pm) Oh, the jokes are
endless here, but though this unique mu-

seum houses a huge collection of penises,
it's actually very well done. From pickled
pickles to petrified wood, there are 286 different members on display, representing all
Icelandic mammals and beyond. Featured
items include contributions from sperm

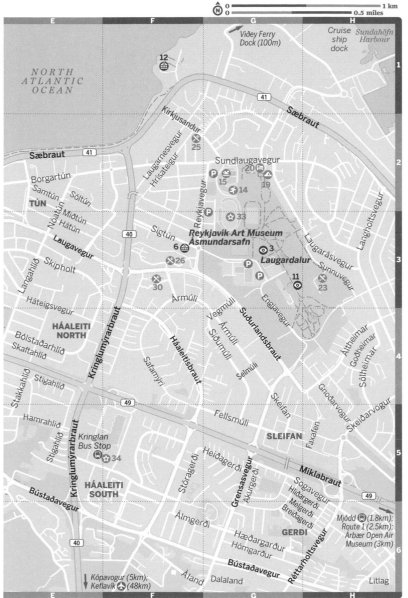

whales and a polar bear, minuscule mouse bits, silver castings of each member of the Icelandic handball team and a single human sample – from deceased mountaineer Páll Arason.

★ **Harpa**   ARTS CENTRE
(p71; Map p82; ☑ box office 528 5050; www.harpa. is; Austurbakki 2; ⊙ 8am-midnight, box office 10am-6pm) With its facets glistening on the water's edge, Reykjavík's sparkling Harpa concert hall and cultural centre is a beauty

77

Reykjavík

to behold. In addition to a season of top-notch shows (some free), it's worth stopping by to explore the shimmering interior with harbour vistas, or take a 45-minute **tour** of the hall (kr1950; 11am, 1.30pm, 3.30pm and 5.30pm daily mid-May to mid-September, 3.30pm Monday to Friday, 11am and 3.30pm Saturday and Sunday rest of the year).

★**Hallgrímskirkja**　　　　　　CHURCH
(p71; Map p82; ☑510 1000; www.hallgrimskirkja. is; Skólavörðustígur; tower adult/child kr900/100; ⊙9am-9pm Jun-Sep, to 5pm Oct-May) Reykjavík's immense white-concrete church (1945–86), star of a thousand postcards, dominates the skyline, and is visible from up to 20km away. Get an unmissable view of the city by taking an elevator up the 74.5m-high **tower**. In contrast to the high drama outside, the Lutheran church's interior is quite plain. The most eye-catching feature is the vast 5275-pipe **organ** installed in 1992. The church's size and radical design caused controversy, and its architect, Guðjón Samúelsson (1887–1950), never saw its completion.

★**Reykjavík Art Museum – Kjarvalsstaðir**　　　　　ART MUSEUM
(p71; Map p76; ☑411 6420; www.artmuseum. is; Flókagata 24, Miklatún Park; adult/child

kr1300/free; ⊙10am-5pm) The angular glass-and-wood Kjarvalsstaðir, which looks out onto **Miklatún Park** (Map p76), is named for Jóhannes Kjarval (1885–1972), one of Iceland's most popular classical artists. He was a fisherman until his crew paid for him to study at the Academy of Fine Arts in Copenhagen, and his wonderfully evocative landscapes share space alongside changing installations of mostly Icelandic 20th-century paintings.

⊙ Old Harbour

Largely a service harbour until recently, the Old Harbour has blossomed into a hot-spot for tourists, with several museums, volcano and Northern Lights films, and excellent restaurants. Whale-watching and puffin-viewing trips depart from the pier. Photo ops abound with views of fishing boats, Harpa concert hall and snowcapped mountains beyond. On the western edge of the harbour, the Grandi area, named after the fish factory there, has burgeoned with eateries and shops as well.

★**Omnom Chocolate**　　　　　FACTORY
(p71; Map p76; ☑519 5959; www.omnom chocolate.com; Hólmaslóð 4, Grandi; adult/child

kr3000/1500; ⏰8am-5pm Mon-Fri) Reserve ahead for a tour at this full-service chocolate factory where you'll see how cocoa beans are transformed into high-end scrumptious delights. The shop sells its bonbons and stylish bars, with specially designed labels and myriad sophisticated flavours. You'll find the bars in shops throughout Iceland.

★ **Kling & Bang** GALLERY
(Map p76; ☑691 4243; http://this.is/klingand bang/; Grandagarður 20, Marshall Húsið, Grandi; ⏰2-6pm Thu-Sun) **FREE** This perennially cutting-edge artist-run exhibition space is a favourite with locals, and now has a new expanded gallery in the renovated Marshall House in the Grandi area near the Old Harbour.

Whales of Iceland MUSEUM
(p71; Map p76; ☑571 0077; www.whalesofice land.is; Fiskislóð 23-25; adult/child kr2900/1500; ⏰10am-6pm Jun-Aug, to 5pm Sep-May; 🚌14) Ever stroll beneath a blue whale? This museum houses full-sized models of the 23 whales found off Iceland's coast. The largest museum of this type in Europe, it also displays models of whale skeletons, and has good audio guides and multimedia screens to explain what you're seeing. It has a cafe and gift shop, online ticket discounts and family tickets (kr5800).

Aurora Reykjavík MUSEUM
(Northern Lights Centre; Map p76; ☑780 4500; www.aurorareykjavik.is; Grandagarður 2; adult/child kr1600/1000; ⏰9am-9pm; 🚌14) Learn about the classical tales explaining the Northern Lights, and the scientific explanation, then watch a 35-minute surround-sound panoramic high-definition recreation of Icelandic auroras.

⊙ **Laugardalur & Around**

Laugardalur encompasses a verdant stretch of land 4km east of the city centre. It was once the main source of Reykjavík's hot-water supply: it translates as 'Hot-Springs Valley', and in the park's centre you'll find relics from the old wash house. The park is a favourite with locals for its huge swimming complex (p80), fed by the geothermal spring, alongside a spa, cafe (p89), skating rink, botanical gardens, sporting and concert arenas, and a kids' zoo/entertainment park.

★ Reykjavík Art
Museum – Ásmundarsafn ART MUSEUM
(p71; Ásmundur Sveinsson Museum; Map p76; ☑411 6430; www.artmuseum.is; Sigtún; adult/child kr1500/free; ⏰10am-5pm May-Sep, 1-5pm Oct-Apr; 🚌2, 5, 15, 17) There's something immensely playful about Ásmundur Sveinsson's (1893–1982) vast collection of sculptures housed in the studio and museum he designed: the rounded, white Ásmundarsafn. Monumental concrete creations fill the garden outside, while the peaceful haven of the interlocking cupolas showcases works in wood, clay and metals, some of them mobile, exploring themes as diverse as folklore and physics. Soaring skylights and white marble give way to a fun dome, where the acoustics create the museum's strict 'must-sing policy'.

Sigurjón Ólafsson Museum ART MUSEUM
(Listasafn Sigurjóns Ólafssonar; Map p76; ☑553 2906; www.lso.is; Laugarnestanga 70; adult/child kr1000/free; ⏰2-5pm Tue-Sun Jun-Aug, 2-5pm Sat & Sun Sep-Nov & Feb-May; 🚌12, 16) Sculptor Sigurjón Ólafsson (1908–82) used this peaceful seafront building as a studio. Now it showcases his varied, powerful work: portrait busts, driftwood totem poles and abstract pillars. A salty ocean breeze blows through the modern rooms, and the area is interlaced with waterfront paths with clear views back to Reykjavík. There are **classical concerts** (kr2500) on Tuesdays in July at 8.30pm. The museum is a branch of the National Gallery; the same ticket covers both.

Reykjavík Botanic Gardens GARDENS
(Grasagarður; Map p76; ☑411 8650; www.grasa gardur.is; Laugardalur; ⏰10am-10pm May-Sep, to 3pm Oct-Apr; 🚌2, 5, 14, 17) **FREE** These gardens contain over 5000 varieties of subarctic plant species, colourful seasonal flowers, the wonderful in-season Café Flóra (p89), and lots of birdlife (particularly grey geese and their fluffy little goslings).

ℹ **THREE FOR THE PRICE OF ONE**

··

The Reykjavík Art Museum ticket covers all three of its sites.

A joint ticket for the National Gallery, nearby Ásgrímur Jónsson Collection and further-afield Sigurjón Ólafsson Museum costs kr1500.

Northern Lights above the city

STRAHL DIMITROV/SHUTTERSTOCK ©

Árbær Open Air Museum　　　MUSEUM
(Árbæjarsafn; www.reykjavikmuseum.is; Kistuhylur 4, Ártúnsholt; adult/child kr1500/free; ⊙10am-5pm Jun-Aug, by tour only 1pm Mon-Fri Sep-May; 🚹; 🚌12, 24) About 20 quaint old buildings have been transported from their original sites to open-air Árbæjarsafn, 4km southeast of the city centre beyond Laugardalur. Alongside 19th-century homes are a turf-roofed church and various stables, smithies, barns and boathouses – all very picturesque. There are summer arts-and-crafts demonstrations and domestic animals, and it's a great place for kids to let off steam. Tours are at 1pm, and there is a cafe.

🏃 Activities

Locally you can tour the city, rent bikes to zoom along lake or seaside trails, or pop into hot-pots all over town. Reykjavík is also the main hub for every kind of activity tour to all manner of destinations beyond the city limits.

⭐Laugardalslaug　　　GEOTHERMAL POOL, HOT-POT
(Map p76; 🗗411 5100; Sundlaugavegur 30a, Laugardalur; adult/child kr900/140, suit/towel rental kr850/570; ⊙6.30am-10pm Mon-Fri, 8am-10pm Sat & Sun; 🚹) One of the largest pools in Iceland, with the best facilities: Olympic-sized indoor pool and outdoor pools, seven hot-pots, a saltwater tub, steam bath and a curling 86m water slide.

⭐Laugar Spa　　　SPA, GYM
(Map p76; 🗗553 0000; www.laugarspa.com; Sundlaugavegur 30a, Laugardalur; day pass kr5490; ⊙6am-11.30pm Mon-Fri, 8am-10pm Sat, to 8pm Sun) Super-duper Laugar Spa, next door to the Laugardalslaug geothermal pool, offers myriad ways to pamper yourself. There are six themed saunas and steam rooms, a sea-water tub, a vast and well-equipped gym, fitness classes, and beauty and massage clinics with detox wraps, facials and hot-stone therapies. The spa is open to visitors over 18 years of age, and entry includes access to Laugardalslaug.

Sundhöllin　　　GEOTHERMAL POOL, HOT-POT
(Map p82; 🗗411 5350; Barónsstígur 16; adult/child kr900/140; ⊙6.30am-10pm Mon-Thu, to 8pm Fri, 8am-4pm Sat, 10am-6pm Sun; 🚹) Reykjavík's oldest swimming pool (1937), designed in art deco style by architect Guðjón Samúelsson, is smack in the city centre and offers the only indoor pool within the city, plus Hallgrímskirkja views from the decks. It's been recently renovated.

Nauthólsvík Geothermal Beach　　　BEACH
(Map p76; 🗗511 6630; www.nautholsvik.is; summer/winter free/kr600, valuables storage summer/winter kr300/free, towel/swimsuit rental kr600/300; ⊙10am-7pm mid-May–mid-Aug, 11am-1pm Mon-Fri, also 5-7.30pm Mon & Wed, 11am-3pm Sat mid-Aug–mid-May; 🚹; 🚌5) The small sandy arc of Nauthólsvík Geothermal Beach, on the edge of the Atlantic, gets

packed on sunny summer days. During opening hours in summer only, geothermal water is routed in to keep the lagoon between 15°C and 19°C. There is also a busy hot-pot (38°C year-round), a snack bar and changing rooms.

Bláfjöll SKIING
(☑561 8400; Blafjallavegur 1; day pass adult/child kr3400/850; ⊘2-9pm Mon-Fri, 10am-5pm Sat & Sun) Iceland's premier ski slopes at 84-sq-km Bláfjöll have 16 lifts, and downhill, cross-country and snowboarding facilities. You can hire gear at reasonable rates. Bláfjöll is about 25km southeast of Reykjavík on Rte 417, just off Rte 1. A shuttle bus (kr1700 return) leaves from the Mjódd bus terminal once daily in season – check with Skíðasvæði (www.skidasvaedi.is) for departure times.

Borgarhjól CYCLING
(Map p82; ☑551 5653; www.borgarhjol.is; Hverfisgata 50; per 4/24hr kr2600/4200; ⊘8am-6pm Mon-Fri, 10am-2pm Sat) Rents and repairs bikes.

📷 Courses

★ Creative Iceland CRAFT
(☑615 3500; www.creativeiceland.is) Get involved with graphic design, cooking, arts, crafts, music…you name it. This service hooks you up with local creative people offering workshops in their art or craft.

🗘 Tours

★ Literary Reykjavík WALKING TOUR
(Map p82; www.bokmenntaborgin.is; Tryggvagata 15; ⊘3pm Thu Jun-Aug) FREE Part of the Unesco City of Literature initiative, free literary walking tours of the city centre start at the main library and include the Dark Deeds tour focusing on crime fiction. There is also a downloadable *Culture Walks* app with several themes.

Atlantsflug FLIGHT TOUR
(☑854 4105; www.flightseeing.is; Reykjavík Domestic Airport) Offers flightseeing tours from Reykjavík, Bakki Airport and Skaftafell. From Reykjavík Domestic Airport you can overfly Eyjafjallajökull crater or Reykjanes Peninsula, or take a day trip with tours around Skaftafell and Jökulsárlón glacial lagoon. Also scheduled flights to Vestmannaeyjar.

Elding Adventures at Sea WHALE WATCHING
(Map p82; ☑519 5000; www.whalewatching.is; Ægisgarður 5; adult/child kr9900/4950; ⊘harbour kiosk 8am-9pm; 🖳14) 🖉 The city's most established and ecofriendly outfit, with an included whale exhibition and refreshments sold on board. Elding also offers angling (adult/child kr13,800/6900) and puffin-watching (adult/child from kr6500/3250) trips and combo tours, and runs the ferry to Viðey. Offers pickup.

Reykjavík Viking Adventure BOAT TOUR
(Map p82; ☑842 6660; www.reykjavikvikingadventure.is; Old Harbour; adult/child kr11,900/6900; ⊘Jun-Aug; 🖳14) Sail in a reconstruction of Viking ship *Gaukstad* from the Old Harbour.

Arctic Adventures ADVENTURE TOUR
(Map p82; ☑562 7000; www.adventures.is; Laugavegur 11; ⊘8am-10pm) With young and enthusiastic staff, this company specialises in action-filled tours: kayaking (kr20,000), rafting (from kr14,000), horse riding, quad-biking, glacier walking (kr11,000) and so on. It has a booking office with gear shop Fjallakofinn (Map p82; ☑510 9505; www.fjallakofinn.is; Laugavegur 11; ⊘9am-7pm Mon-Fri, 10am-5pm Sat, noon-6pm Sun) in central Reykjavík.

⭐ Festivals & Events

★ Iceland Airwaves MUSIC
(www.icelandairwaves.is; ⊘Nov) You'd be forgiven for thinking Iceland is just one giant

---

LOCAL KNOWLEDGE

POOLS & HOT-POTS

Reykjavík's naturally hot water is the heart of the city's social life (as in many Icelandic towns); children play, teenagers flirt, business deals are made and everyone catches up on the latest gossip at the baths. Volcanic heat keeps the temperature at a mellow 29°C, and most baths have *heitir pottar* (hot-pots): jacuzzi-like pools kept a toasty 37°C to 42°C. Bring towels and bathing suits or rent them on-site. For further information and more locations, see www.spacity.is.

Reykjavikers get very upset by dirty tourists in their clean, chemical-free pools. To avoid causing huge offence, you must wash thoroughly with soap and without a swimsuit before hopping in.

Central Reykjavík

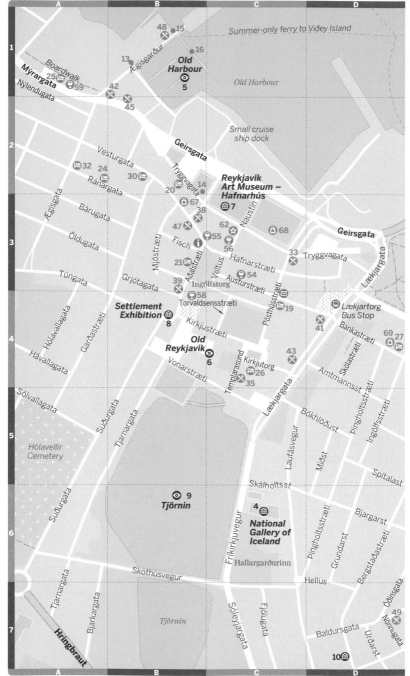

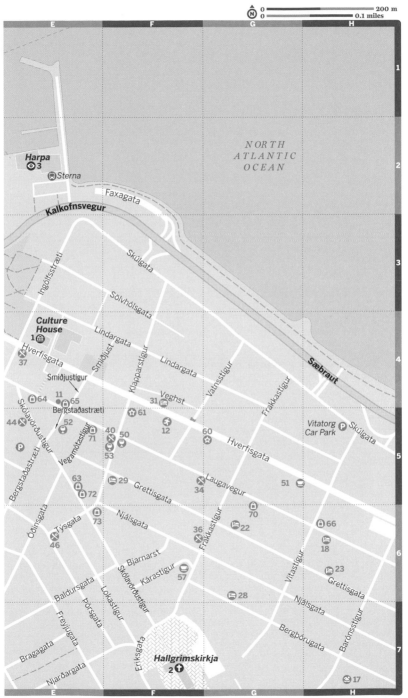

North Atlantic Ocean

Harpa
⊙3

🚌Sterna

Faxagata

Kalkofnsvegur

Skúlagata

Sölvhólsgata

Ingólfsstræti

Culture
House
1🏛

Hverfisgata
❌37

Lindargata

Smiðjust.

Klapparstígur

Lindargata

Vatnsstígur

Frakkastígur

Sæbraut

Smiðjustígur

11
🔒64 🔒65

Bergstaðastræti

Veghst
🔒31 🍴

❌44

🔒52

⭐61

🍴12

60
⭐

Hverfisgata

Vitatorg P Skúlagata
Car Park

🔒40 50
🔒71 ❌53 🍴

P

Skólavörðustígur

Bergstaðastræti

Vegamótastígur

🔒63 🔒72

🍴29 Grettisgata

❌34 Laugavegur

51🚌

🔒73

Njálsgata

70
🔒

Óðinsgata

Týsgata
❌46

🔒66

🍴22
36
❌ Frakkastígur

🍴18

Bjarnarst

Skólavörðustígur

Kárastígur

🍴57

Vitastígur

🍴23 Grettisgata

Njálsgata

🍴28

Baldursgata

Lokastígur

Þórsgata

Freyjugata

Bragagata

Njarðargata

Eiríksgata

Barónsstígur

Bergþórugata

Hallgrímskirkja
2✝

🏊17

83

Central Reykjavík

music-producing machine. Since the first edition of Iceland Airwaves was held in 1999, this fab festival has become one of the world's premier annual showcases for new music (Icelandic and otherwise).

★ **Secret Solstice**   MUSIC
(www.secretsolstice.is; ☉ Jun) This excellent music festival with local and international acts coincides with the summer solstice, so there's 24-hour daylight for partying. It's held at Reykjavík's Laugardalur.

★ **Reykjavík Culture Night**   CULTURAL
(www.menningarnott.is; ☉ Aug) On Menningarnótt, held mid-month, Reykjavikers turn out in force for a day and night of art, music, dance and fireworks. Many galleries, ateliers, shops, cafes and churches stay open until late. Your chance to get sporty and sophisticated on the one day: this event is held on the same date as the city's marathon.

**Reykjavík International
Film Festival**   FILM
(www.riff.is; ⊗ Sep-Oct) This intimate 11-day
event from late September features quirky
programming that highlights independent film-making, both homegrown and
international.

🛏 Sleeping

⭐**Loft Hostel**   HOSTEL €
(Map p82; 🕿 553 8140; www.lofthostel.is;
Bankastræti 7; dm kr7600-8700, d/q kr27,800/
37,600; @ 🛜) Perched high above the action
on bustling Bankastræti, this modern hostel
attracts a decidedly young crowd, including locals who come for its trendy bar and
cafe terrace. This sociable spot comes with
prim dorms, linen included and en suite
bathrooms in each. HI members discount
kr700/2800 for a dorm/double.

⭐**Reykjavík Downtown Hostel**   HOSTEL €
(Map p82; 🕿 553 8120; www.hostel.is; Vesturgata 17; dm 4-/10-bed kr9100/6450, d with/
without bathroom kr27,800/23,800; @ 🛜)
Squeaky clean and well run, this effortlessly charming hostel gets such good reviews
that it regularly lures large groups and the
nonbackpacker set. Enjoy friendly service,
guest kitchen and excellent rooms. Discount
kr700 for HI members.

Reykjavík City Hostel   HOSTEL €
(Map p76; 🕿 553 8110; www.hostel.is; Sundlaugavegur 34; dm from kr4750, d with/without
bathroom kr17,900/12,900; 🅿 @ 🛜) 🏄 Reykjavík's original hostel is a large, ecofriendly
complex with a fun backpacker vibe.
Two kilometres east of the city centre in
Laugardalur, it abuts the campground and
swimming pool, and is served by the Flybus and many tour operators. It boasts bike
rental, three guest kitchens and a spacious
deck. There's a kr700 discount for HI members, and kids four to 12 years get a kr1500
discount.

Oddsson Hostel   HOSTEL €
(Map p76; 🕿 511 3579; www.oddsson.is; Hring-
braut 121; dm/pod kr5600/7500, d with/without
bathroom kr35,000/22,000; 🛜; 🖵 14) You can't
miss this large, quirky new hostel near the
Old Harbour neighbourhood with its brightly coloured facade. There are dorm rooms,
tiny private pods and hotel rooms with
shared or private bathrooms, some with excellent sea views. Everyone shares a kitch-
en, hot tub, rooftop, and yoga and karaoke

rooms. A good restaurant-bar called Bazaar
rounds it out.

Reykjavík Campsite   CAMPGROUND €
(Map p76; 🕿 568 6944; www.reykjavikcampsite.
is; Sundlaugavegur 32; sites per adult/child kr2100/
free, cabin kr14,000; ⊗ May-Sep; 🅿 @ 🛜) 🏄
Reykjavík's only campground (2km east of
the city centre in Laugardalur, next to the
swimming pool and City Hostel) is popular
in summer with campers. There's space for
650 people in three fields, so you're likely to
find a spot. Extensive, modern facilities include small cabins (three-night minimum),
free showers, bike hire (five hours kr3500),
kitchens and barbecue areas.

⭐**REY Apartments**   APARTMENT €€
(Map p82; 🕿 771 4600; www.rey.is; Grettisgata
2a; apt kr23,000-49,800; 🛜) For those lean-
ing towards private digs rather than hotel
stays, REY is a very handy choice with a
huge cache of modern apartments scattered
across several Escher-like stairwells. They're
well maintained and stylishly decorated.

⭐**Nest Apartments**   APARTMENT €€
(Map p82; 🕿 893 0280; http://nestapartments.
is; Bergthorugata 15; apt from kr21,100; 🛜) Four
thoroughly modern apartments with neat
antique touches make a superb home away
from home on a peaceful residential street
just north of Hallgrímskirkja. In a tall town
house, each apartment has a different lay-
out, and the largest sleeps four people. Two-
night minimum.

**Forsæla
Apartmenthouse**   GUESTHOUSE, APARTMENT €€
(Map p82; 🕿 551 6046; www.apartmenthouse.
is; Grettisgata 33b; d/tr without bathroom incl
breakfast kr22,700/30,800, apt/house from
kr38,200/74,000; 🛜) This lovely option in
Reykjavík's centre stars a 100-year-old
wood-and-tin house for four to eight people, which comes with all the old beams and
tasteful mod cons you could want. Three
apartments have small, cosy bedrooms and
sitting rooms, kitchens and washing machines. Plus there's B&B lodging with shared
bathrooms. Minimum three-night stay in
apartments and the house.

Galtafell Guesthouse   GUESTHOUSE €€
(Map p76; 🕿 551 4344; www.galtafell.com;
Laufásvegur 46; d with/without bathroom from
kr25,300/22,100, apt from kr26,000; 🛜) In a
quiet lakeside neighbourhood within easy
walking distance of the city centre, the four

one-bedroom apartments in this converted historic mansion contain fully equipped kitchens and cosy seating areas. Three doubles share a guest kitchen. The garden and entry spaces feel suitably lovely.

Grettisborg Apartments   APARTMENT €€
(Map p82; ☑666 0655; www.grettisborg.is; Grettisgata 51; apt kr21,200-51,500; 🛜) Like sleeping in a magazine for Scandinavian home design, these thoroughly modern studios and apartments sport fine furnishings and sleek built-ins. The largest sleeps six or seven.

Guesthouse Butterfly   GUESTHOUSE €€
(Map p82; ☑894 1864; www.butterfly.is; Ránargata 8a; d with/without bathroom incl breakfast kr24,500/18,250; 🛜) On a quiet, central residential street, you can't miss Butterfly's flamboyant mural. Neat, simply furnished rooms, a guest kitchen and friendly Icelandic-Norwegian owners make you feel right at home. Self-contained apartments (from kr27,000) with kitchen and some with balcony are great for the family.

Three Sisters   APARTMENT €€
(Þrjár Systur; Map p82; ☑565 2181; www. threesisters.is; Ránargata 16; apt from kr25,700; ☺mid-May–Aug; @🛜) A twinkly-eyed former fisherman runs the Three Sisters, a corner town house in old Reykjavík, now divided into eight studio apartments. Comfy beds are flanked by homey decor and flat-screen TVs. Each studio has a kitchen.

CenterHótel Plaza   HOTEL €€
(Map p82; ☑595 8550; www.plaza.is; Aðalstræti 4; d incl breakfast from kr28,300; @🛜) A full-service hotel in an enviably central spot in the Old Reykjavík quarter, this bland member of the CenterHótel chain

has business-oriented rooms with polished wooden floors, and great views from the higher levels.

★**Reykjavík Residence**   APARTMENT €€€
(Map p82; ☑561 1200; www.rrhotel.is; Hverfisgata 45; apt kr33,300-70,200; @🛜) Plush city-centre living feels just right in these two converted historic mansions. Linens are crisp, service is attentive and the light a glowing gold. They come in loads of configurations from suites and studios with kitchenettes to two- and three-bedroom apartments.

★**Black Pearl**   APARTMENT €€€
(Map p82; ☑527 9600; www.blackpearlreykjavik. com; Tryggvagata 18 & 18c; apt kr54,600-144,000; Ⓟ@🛜) These 10 fully kitted-out apartments fill several black towers just back from the waterfront. Full-service reception provides personal attention (maid service, laundry, child care), but spacious, cleanly decorated apartments that sleep two to six offer independence. Think king-sized beds, designer furniture and balconies, some with water views.

Kvosin Downtown Hotel   APARTMENT €€€
(Map p82; ☑415 2400; www.kvosinhotel.is; Kirkjutorg 4; apt incl breakfast from kr46,200; 🛜) Firmly a part of the luxury-apartment wave, these superbly located mod pads range from 'Big' and 'Bigger' to 'Mountain Suite'. Nespresso machines adorn the kitchenettes and all the mod cons are standard, including Sóley Organics toiletries. The Mountain Suite has amazing balconies.

Apotek   BOUTIQUE HOTEL €€€
(Map p82; ☑512 9000; www.keahotels.is; Austurstræti 16; d incl breakfast from kr44,100; 🛜) This new hotel in a well-renovated 1917 Guðjón Samúelsson building, a former pharmacy, smack in the centre of Old Reykjavík offers slick contemporary rooms in muted tones and a popular ground-floor tapas-style restaurant-bar (p91) as well.

Alda Hotel   BOUTIQUE HOTEL €€€
(Map p82; ☑553 9366; www.aldahotel.is; Laugavegur 66-68; d from kr34,300; 🛜) This smart player on Reykjavík's city-centre hotel scene offers sleek rooms with all the mod cons, including a spa and fitness centre and a spacious lounge. All of the deluxe 4th-floor rooms have balconies, suites often have two bathrooms, and some rooms have ocean views.

Icelandair Hotel
Reykjavík Marina BOUTIQUE HOTEL €€€
(Map p82; ☎560 8000; www.icelandairhotels.
is; Mýrargata 2; d kr38,900-49,900; @ ☎)
This large design hotel on the Old Harbour is decked out in captivating art, cool
nautical-chic decor elements and up-to-the-
second mod cons. Clever ways to conserve
space make small rooms winners overall.
Attic rooms on the harbour side have excellent sea views. The lively lobby sports a live
satellite feed to sights all over Iceland, and
the happening Slippbarinn (p93).

🍴 Eating

⭐**Sægreifinn** SEAFOOD €
(Seabaron; Map p82; ☎553 1500; www.
saegreifinn.is; Geirsgata 8; mains kr1350-1900;
⊙11.30am-11pm mid-May–Aug, to 10pm Sep–mid-
May) Sidle into this green harbourside shack
for the most famous lobster soup (kr1350) in
the capital, or to choose from a fridge full of
fresh fish skewers to be grilled on the spot.
Though the original sea baron sold the restaurant some years ago, the place retains a
homey, laid-back feel.

⭐**Frú Lauga** MARKET €
(Map p76; ☎534 7165; www.frulauga.is;
Laugalækur 6; ⊙11am-6pm Mon-Fri, to 4pm Sat;

🍴) 🥕 Reykjavík's trailblazing farmers
market sources its ingredients from all
over the countryside, featuring treats like
skyr (yoghurtlike dessert) from the town
of Erpsstaðir, organic vegetables, rhubarb
conserves, meats, honey, and a range of
carefully curated international pastas,
chocolates, wine and the like. It also operates a cafe at Reykjavík Art Museum – Hafnarhús (p74).

⭐**Stofan Kaffihús** CAFE €
(Map p82; ☎546 1842; www.facebook.com/
stofan.cafe/; Vesturgata 3; dishes kr1500-1600;
⊙9am-11pm Mon-Wed, to midnight Thu-Sat,
10am-10pm Sun; ☎) This laid-back cafe
in a historic brick building has a warm
feel with its worn wooden floors, plump
couches and spacious main room. Settle
in for coffee, cake or soup, and watch the
world go by.

Valdi's ICE CREAM €
(Map p76; ☎586 8088; www.valdis.is; Grandagarður 21; scoops kr450; ⊙11.30am-11pm May-
Aug; 👶) Throughout summer happy families
flock here, take a number and join the crush
waiting for a scoop chosen from the huge array of homemade ice creams. Totally casual,
totally fun.

DON'T MISS

THE BLUE LAGOON

In a magnificent black-lava field, the milky-teal Blue Lagoon spa is fed water from the
futuristic Svartsengi geothermal plant; with its silver towers, roiling clouds of steam
and people daubed in white silica mud, it's an otherworldly place. Those who say it's too
commercial and too crowded aren't wrong, but you'll be missing something special if you
don't go. Prebooking is essential.

The superheated water (70% sea water, 30% fresh water, at a perfect 38°C) is rich
in blue-green algae, mineral salts and fine silica mud, which condition and exfoliate the
skin – sounds like advertising speak, but you really do come out as soft as a baby's bum.
The water is hottest near the vents where it emerges, and the surface is several degrees
warmer than the bottom.

The lagoon has been developed for visitors with an enormous, modern complex of
changing rooms, restaurants, a rooftop viewpoint and a gift shop. It's landscaped with
hot-pots, steam rooms, a sauna, a bar and a piping-hot waterfall that delivers a powerful
hydraulic massage – like being pummelled by a troll. A VIP section has its own interior
wading space, lounge and viewing platform. Construction of an expanded spa and five-
star hotel is due to be completed in 2017. You must book spa treatments well in advance.
Towel or bathing-suit hire is €5.

The lagoon is 47km southwest of Reykjavík and 23km southeast of Keflavík International Airport. The complex is just off the road between Keflavík and Grindavík. Bus services run year-round, as do tours (which sometimes offer better deals than a bus ticket
plus lagoon admission). You must book in advance. If your bus or tour does not include
lagoon entry, you must prebook at www.bluelagoon.com.

Bakarí Sandholt BAKERY €
(Map p82; ☎551 3524; www.sandholt.is; Laugavegur 36; snacks kr600-1200; ⏱7am-9pm; 📶) Reykjavík's favourite bakery is usually crammed with folks hoovering up the generous assortment of fresh baguettes, croissants, pastries and sandwiches. The soup of the day (kr1540) comes with delicious sourdough bread.

Brauð & Co BAKERY €
(Map p82; www.braudogco.is; Frakkastígur 16; ⏱6am-6pm Mon-Fri, to 5pm Sat & Sun) Queue for some of the city's best home-baked breads and pastries at this tiny new bakery where you can watch Viking hipsters make the goodies while you wait.

Hamborgara Búllan BURGERS €
(Hamborgarabúlla Tómasar; Map p82; ☎511 1888; www.bullan.is; Geirsgata 1; mains kr1200-1800; ⏱11.30am-9pm; 📶👪) The Old Harbour's outpost of burgerdom and Americana proffers savoury patties that are perennial local favourites. Russell Crowe was spotted here while filming in 2012.

Burið CHEESE €
(Map p76; ☎551 8400; http://blog.burid.is; Grandagarður 35; ⏱11am-6pm Mon-Fri, noon-5pm Sat; 🚌14) Select from a broad range of Icelandic cheeses, *skyr* and other deli and sweet treats.

Walk the Plank SEAFOOD €
(Map p82; www.facebook.com/walktheplankiceland; Ægisgarður; mains kr1500-1900; ⏱10am-8pm) On decent-weather days and around whale-watching departures, this tiny food truck opens its window and dishes up yummy crab-cake sliders on the quay.

Bæjarins Beztu HOT DOGS €
(Map p82; www.bbp.is; Tryggvagata; hot dogs kr420; ⏱10am-2am Sun-Thu, to 4.30am Fri & Sat; 👪) Icelanders swear the city's best hot dogs are at this truck near the harbour (patronised by Bill Clinton and late-night bar-hoppers). Use the vital sentence *Eina með öllu* (One with everything) to get the quintessential favourite with sweet mustard, ketchup and crunchy onions.

★**Messinn** SEAFOOD €€
(Map p82; ☎546 0095; www.messinn.com; Lækjargata 6b; lunch mains kr1900-2100, dinner mains kr2500-3800; ⏱11.30am-3pm & 5-10pm; 📶) Make a beeline to Messinn for the best seafood that Reykjavík has to offer. The speciality is amazing pan-fries where your pick of fish is served up in a sizzling cast-iron skillet accompanied by buttery potatoes and salad. The mood is upbeat and comfortable, and the staff friendly.

★**Matur og Drykkur** ICELANDIC €€
(Map p76; ☎571 8877; www.maturogdrykkur.is; Grandagarður 2; lunch mains kr1900-3200, dinner menus kr3000-5000; ⏱11.30am-3pm Mon-Sat, 6-10.30pm Tue-Sat; 🚌14) One of Reykjavík's top high-concept restaurants, Matur Og Drykkur means 'Food and Drink', and you surely will be plied with the best of both. It's the brainchild of brilliant chef Gísli Matthías Auðunsson, who also owns excellent Slippurinn (p32) in the Vestmannaeyjar, and

WORTH A TRIP

VIÐEY

On fine-weather days, the tiny uninhabited island of **Viðey** (www.reykjavikmuseum.is) makes a wonderful day trip. Just 1km north of Reykjavík's Sundahöfn Harbour, it feels a world away. Well-preserved historic buildings, surprising modern art, an abandoned village and great birdwatching add to its remote spell. The only sounds are the wind, the waves and the golden bumblebees buzzing among the tufted vetch and hawkweed.

The whole island is criss-crossed with walking paths. Some you can bicycle, others are more precarious. When boats are running from the Old Harbour, you can hire a bike there at Reykjavík Bike Tours (p95) and bring it to the island.

There is no accommodation and just one mediocre cafe on the island: bring supplies to picnic or barbecue at the Viðeyjarnaust day-hut.

The **Viðey Ferry** (☎533 5055; www.videy.com; return adult/child kr1200/600; ⏱from Skarfabakki hourly 10.15am-5.15pm mid-May–Sep, weekends only Oct–mid-May) takes five minutes from Skarfabakki, 4.5km east of the city centre. During summer, two boats a day start from Elding at the Old Harbour and the Harpa concert hall. Bus 16 stops closest to Skarfabakki.

Blue Lagoon (p87)

creates inventive versions of traditional Icelandic fare. Book ahead in high season and for dinner.

Café Flóra
CAFE €€

(Flóran; Map p76; ☑ 553 8872; www.floran.is; Botanic Gardens; cakes kr950, mains kr1400-3000; ⊗10am-10pm May-Sep; ☑) ✐ Sun-dappled tables fill a greenhouse in the Botanic Gardens and spill onto a flower-lined terrace at this lovely cafe that specialises in wholesome local ingredients – some grown in the gardens themselves! Soups come with fantastic sourdough bread, and snacks range from cheese platters with nuts and honey to pulled-pork sandwiches. Weekend brunch, good coffee and homemade cakes round it all out.

Gló
ORGANIC, VEGETARIAN €€

(Map p82; ☑ 553 1111; www.glo.is; Laugavegur 20b; mains kr1200-2000; ⊗11am-10pm Mon-Fri, 11.30am-10pm Sat & Sun; ☜☑) ✐ Join the cool cats in this upstairs, airy restaurant serving fresh, large daily specials loaded with Asian-influenced herbs and spices. Though not exclusively vegetarian, it's a wonderland of raw and organic foods with your choice from a broad bar of elaborate salads, from root veggies to Greek. It also has branches in **Laugardalur** (Map p76; ☑ 553 1111; Engjateigur 19; ⊗11am-9pm Mon-Fri; ☜☑) and **Kópavogur** (Hæðasmári 6; ⊗11am-9pm Mon-Fri, 11.30am-9pm Sat & Sun; ☜☑).

Snaps
FRENCH €€

(Map p82; ☑ 511 6677; www2.snaps.is; Þórsgata 1; dinner mains kr3800-5000; ⊗7-10am daily, 11.30am-11pm Sun-Thu, to midnight Fri & Sat) Reserve ahead for this French bistro that's a mega-hit with locals. Snaps' secret is simple: serve tasty seafood and classic bistro mains – think steak or *moules frites* – at surprisingly decent prices.

Coocoo's Nest
CAFE €€

(Map p76; ☑ 552 5454; www.coocoosnest.is; Grandagarður 23; mains kr1700-4500; ⊗11am-10pm Tue-Sat, to 4pm Sun; ☜) Pop into this cool eatery tucked behind the Old Harbour for popular weekend brunches (dishes kr1700 to kr2200; 11am to 4pm Friday to Sunday) paired with decadent cocktails (kr1300). Casual, small and groovy, with mosaic plywood tables; the menu changes and there are nightly themes, but it's always scrumptious.

Ostabúðin
DELI €€

(Cheese Shop; Map p82; ☑ 562 2772; www.face book.com/Ostabudin/; Skólavörðustígur 8; mains kr3600-5000; ⊗restaurant 11.30am-9pm Mon-Fri, noon-9pm Sat & Sun, deli 10am-6pm Mon-Thu, to 7pm Fri, 11am-4pm Sat) Head to this gourmet cheese shop and deli with a large dining room for the friendly owner's cheese and meat platters (from kr1900 to kr4000), or the catch of the day with homemade bread. You can pick up other local goods, like terrines and duck confit, on the way out.

89

WHALE, SHARK & PUFFIN

Many restaurants and tour operators in Iceland tout their more unusual delicacies: whale (*hvál/hvalur*), shark (fermented and called *hákarl*) and puffin (*lundi*). Before you dig in, consider that what may have been sustainable with 332,000 Icelanders becomes taxing on species and delicate ecosystems when 1,300,000 tourists annually get involved. Be aware:

➡ As much as an estimated 40% to 60% of Icelandic whale meat consumption is by tourists

➡ A total of 82% of Icelanders never eat whale meat

➡ Only 3% of Icelanders eat whale regularly

➡ Between 75% and 85% of minke whale is thrown away after killing

➡ Fin whales are classified as endangered globally; their status in the North Atlantic is hotly debated

➡ Iceland's Ministry of Industries and Innovation maintains the whale catch is sustainable, at less than 1% of local stock, despite international protest

➡ The Greenland shark, which is used for *hákarl*, has a conservation status of 'near threatened' globally

➡ In 2002 there were an estimated seven million puffins in Iceland, in 2015 there were about four million – a 43% drop, with much more among juveniles (a 65% drop) due to consistently poor chick production

➡ At the time of writing, Icelandic puffins were experiencing an enormous breeding failure in their largest colonies, in the Vestmannaeyjar Islands

While we do not exclude restaurants that serve these meats from our listings, you can opt not to order the meat, or easily find whale-free spots at www.icewhale.is/whale-friendly-restaurants.

Bergsson Mathús   CAFE €€
(Map p82; ☑ 571 1822; www.bergsson.is; Templarasund 3; mains kr2000-2400; ⊙7am-9pm Mon-Fri, to 5pm Sat & Sun; ☑) This popular, no-nonsense cafe features homemade breads, fresh produce and filling lunch specials. Stop by on weekends when locals flip through magazines, gossip and devour delicious brunch plates. After 4pm there is two-for-one takeaway.

Hverfisgata 12   PIZZERIA €€
(Map p82; ☑ 437 0203; www.hverfisgata12.is; Hverfisgata 12; pizzas kr2450-3400; ⊙5pm-1am Mon-Thu, 11.30am-1am Fri-Sun; ☑) There's no sign, but those in the know come to this cream-coloured corner house for some of the city's best pizzas with fabulous family-style ambience. Cheerful staff work behind the copper bar, and round tables fill bay windows. Weekend brunches are a big draw, too.

Bryggjan Brugghús   PUB FOOD €€
(Map p76; ☑ 456 4040; www.bryggjanbrugghus.is; Grandagarður 8; mains kr2300-5000; ⊙11am-midnight Sun-Thu, to 1am Sat & Sun, kitchen 11.30am-11pm; ☑) This enormous, golden-lit microbrewery and bistro is a welcome respite for one of its home-brewed beers (start with IPA, lager and seasonal beers, from 12 taps) or for an extensive menu of seafood and meat dishes, and occasional DJs. You've also got great harbour views out the back windows. Settle in for a while.

Restó   SEAFOOD €€
(Map p76; ☑ 546 9550; www.resto.is; Rauðarárstígur 27-29; mains kr3600-5000; ⊙5.30-10pm Sun-Thu, to 10.30pm Fri & Sat) This homey little restaurant is over by Hlemmur Sq but it's worth the trek for delicious changing menus of seafood, and the friendly family who runs the place. The owner-chef Jóhann Helgi Jóhannesson was the chef at celebrated seafood joint Ostabúðin, and he and his wife, Ragnheiður Helena Eðvarðsdóttir, have created a new anchor in this up-and-coming district.

⭐ Dill
ICELANDIC €€€

(Map p82; ☎552 1522; www.dillrestaurant. is; Hverfisgata 12; 5-course meal from kr11,900; ⏱6-10pm Wed-Sat) Top New Nordic cuisine is the major drawcard at this elegant yet simple bistro. The focus is very much on the food – locally sourced produce served as a parade of courses. The owners are friends with Copenhagen's famous Noma clan, and take Icelandic cuisine to similarly heady heights. Popular with locals and visitors alike, a reservation is a must.

⭐ Þrír Frakkar
ICELANDIC, SEAFOOD €€€

(Map p82; ☎552 3939; www.3frakkar.com; Baldursgata 14; mains kr4000-6000; ⏱11.30am-2.30pm & 6-10pm Mon-Fri, 6-11pm Sat & Sun) Owner-chef Úlfar Eysteinsson has built up a consistently excellent reputation at this snug little restaurant – apparently a favourite of Jamie Oliver's. Specialities range throughout the aquatic world from salt cod and halibut to *plokkfiskur* (fish stew) with black bread. Nonfish items run towards guillemot, horse, lamb and whale.

Fiskfélagið
SEAFOOD €€€

(Map p82; ☎552 5300; www.fishcompany.is; Vesturgata 2a; mains lunch kr2400-3000, dinner kr4900-6000; ⏱11.30am-2.30pm Mon-Sat, 5.30-11pm Sun-Thu, to 11.30pm Fri & Sat) The 'Fish Company' takes Icelandic seafood recipes and spins them through a variety of far-flung inspirations, from Fiji coconut to Spanish chorizo. Dine in an intimate-feeling stone-and-timber room with copper light fittings and quirky furnishings or out on the terrace.

Fiskmarkaðurinn
SEAFOOD €€€

(Fishmarket; Map p82; ☎578 8877; www.fisk markadurinn.is; Aðalstræti 12; mains kr5100-5700; ⏱6-11.30pm) This restaurant excels in infusing Icelandic seafood and local produce with unique flavours like lotus root. The tasting menu (kr11,900) is tops, and it is renowned for its excellent sushi bar (kr3600 to kr4600).

Apotek
FUSION €€€

(Map p82; ☎551 0011; www.apotekrestaurant. is; Austurstræti 16; mains kr3000-8000; ⏱11.30am-1am) This beautiful restaurant and bar with shining glass fixtures and a cool ambience is equally known for its delicious menu of small plates, perfect for sharing, and its top-flight cocktails. It's on the ground floor of the hotel of the same name (p86).

Grillmarkaðurinn
FUSION €€€

(Grill Market; Map p82; ☎571 7777; www.grill markadurinn.is; Lækargata 2a; mains kr4600-7000; ⏱11.30am-2pm Mon-Fri, 6-10.30pm Sun-Thu, to 11.30pm Fri & Sat) Tip-top dining is the order of the day here, from the moment you enter the glass atrium with the golden-globe lights to your first snazzy cocktail, and on through the meal. Service is impeccable, and locals and visitors alike rave about the food: locally sourced Icelandic ingredients prepared with culinary imagination by master chefs.

Vox
ICELANDIC €€€

(Map p76; ☎444 5050; www.vox.is; Suður-landsbraut 2; mains kr4200-7000, lunch buffet kr3650, brunch kr3950; ⏱11.30am-10.30pm) The Hilton's five-star restaurant has a contemporary but welcoming vibe and continues to pack 'em in for New Nordic cuisine and a famous weekend brunch.

🍷 Drinking & Nightlife

Sometimes it's hard to distinguish between cafes, restaurants and bars in Reykjavík, because when night rolls around (whether light or dark out) many coffeeshops and bistros turn lights down and volume up, swapping cappuccinos for cocktails.

⭐ Kaffibarinn
BAR

(Map p82; www.kaffibarinn.is; Bergstaðastræti 1; ⏱3pm-1am Sun-Thu, to 4.30am Fri & Sat; 🛜) This old house with the London Underground symbol over the door contains one of Reykjavík's coolest bars; it even had a starring role in the cult movie *101 Reykjavík* (2000). At weekends you'll feel like you need a famous face or a battering ram to get in. At other times it's a place for artistic types to chill with their Macs.

⭐ Micro Bar
BAR

(Map p82; www.facebook.com/MicroBarIceland/; Vesturgata 2; ⏱2pm-12.30am Sun-Thu, to 2am Fri & Sat) Boutique brews are the name of the game at this low-key spot in the heart of the action. Bottles of beer represent a slew of brands and countries, but more importantly you'll discover 10 local draughts on tap from the island's top microbreweries: one of the best selections in Reykjavík. Happy hour (5pm to 7pm) offers kr850 beers.

Kaldi BAR

(Map p82; www.kaldibar.is; Laugavegur 20b; ⊗noon-1am Sun-Thu, to 3am Fri & Sat) Effortlessly cool with mismatched seats and teal banquettes, plus a popular smoking courtyard, Kaldi is awesome for its full range of Kaldi microbrews, not available elsewhere. Happy hour (4pm to 7pm) gets you one for kr700. Anyone can play the in-house piano.

Loftið COCKTAIL BAR

(Map p82; ☑551 9400; www.loftidbar.is; 2nd fl, Austurstræti 9; ⊗2pm-1am Sun-Thu, 4pm-3am Fri & Sat) Loftið is all about high-end cocktails and good living. Dress up to join the fray at this airy upstairs lounge with a zinc bar, retro tailor-shop-inspired decor, vintage tiles and a swank, older crowd. The basic booze here is the top-shelf liquor elsewhere, and jazzy bands play from time to time.

Paloma CLUB

(Map p82; www.facebook.com/BarPaloma/; Naustin 1-3; ⊗8pm-1am Thu & Sun, to 4.30am Fri & Sat; ⊞) One of Reykjavík's best late-night dance clubs, with DJs upstairs laying down reggae, electronica and pop, and a dark deep house dance scene in the basement.

Kaffi Vínyl CAFE

(Map p82; ☑537 1332; www.facebook.com/vin ilrvk/; Hverfisgata 76; ⊗9am-11pm Mon-Fri, 10am-11pm Sat, noon-11pm Sun; ⊛) This new entry on the Reykjavík coffee, restaurant and music scene is popular for its chill vibe, great music, and delicious vegan and vegetarian food.

Mikkeller & Friends CRAFT BEER

(Map p82; www.mikkeller.dk; Hverfisgata 12; ⊗5pm-1am Sun-Thu, 2pm-1am Fri & Sat; ⊛) Climb to the top floor of the building shared by excellent pizzeria Hverfisgata 12 and you'll find this Danish craft-beer pub. Its 20 taps rotate through Mikkeller's own offerings and local Icelandic craft beers. The vibe is laid-back and colourful.

Reykjavík Roasters CAFE

(Map p82; www.reykjavikroasters.is; Kárastígur 1; ⊗8am-6pm Mon-Fri, 9am-5pm Sat & Sun) These

---

LOCAL KNOWLEDGE

DJAMMIÐ: HOW TO PARTY IN REYKJAVÍK

Reykjavík is renowned for its weekend party scene that goes strong into the wee hours, and even spills over onto some of the weekdays (especially in summer). *Djammið* in the capital means going out on the town, or you could say *pöbbarölt* for a 'pub stroll'. (This should not be confused with the infamous countryside *rúntur*, which involves Icelandic youth driving around their town in one big automotive party.)

Much of Reykjavík's partying happens in cafes and bistros that transform into raucous beer-soaked bars on weekends, and at the many dedicated pubs and clubs. But it's not the quantity of drinking dens that makes Reykjavík's nightlife special – it's the upbeat energy that pours from them.

Thanks to the high price of alcohol, things generally don't get going until late. Icelanders brave the melee at the government alcohol store **Vínbúðin** (www.vinbudin.is), then toddle home for a prepub party. Once they're merry, people hit town around midnight, party until 5am, queue for a hot dog, then topple into bed or the gutter, whichever is more convenient. Considering the quantity of booze swilling, the scene is pretty good-natured.

Rather than settling into one venue for the evening, Icelanders like to cruise from bar to bar, getting progressively louder and less inhibited as the evening goes on. 'In' clubs may have long queues, but they tend to move quickly with the constant circulation of revellers.

Most of the action is concentrated near Laugavegur and Austurstræti. Places usually stay open until 1am Sunday to Thursday and 4am or 5am on Friday and Saturday. You'll pay around kr1000 to kr1600 per pint of beer, and cocktails hit the kr1800 to kr2600 mark. Some venues have cover charges (around kr1000) after midnight, and many have early-in-the-evening happy hours that cut costs to kr500 or kr700 per beer; download smartphone app *Reykjavík Appy Hour*.

Things change fast – check *Grapevine* (www.grapevine.is) for the latest listings. You should dress up to fit in, although there are some more relaxed pub-style joints. The legal drinking age is 20 years.

folks take their coffee seriously. This tiny hipster joint is easily spotted on warm days with its smattering of wooden tables on a small square. Swig a perfect latte with a flaky croissant. It now has a branch (Map p76; Brautarholt 2; ☺8am-6pm Mon-Fri, 9am-5pm Sat & Sun; ☎) in the Hlemmur area.

Skúli Craft Bar CRAFT BEER
(Map p82; ☑519 6455; Aðalstræti 9; ☺2-11pm Sun-Thu, to 1am Fri & Sat) Loads of draught and bottled beers (130 at last count) served with a smile in a welcoming brick and beam sort of place. Six-beer flight costs kr3100.

Slippbarinn COCKTAIL BAR
(Map p82; ☑560 8080; www.slippbarinn.is; Mýrargata 2; ☺noon-midnight Sun-Thu, to 1am Fri & Sat; ☎) Jet setters unite at this buzzy restaurant (mains kr2900 to kr5000) and bar at the Old Harbour in the Icelandair Hotel Reykjavík Marina (p87). It's bedecked with vintage record players and chatting locals sipping some of the best cocktails in town.

Bike Cave CAFE
(Map p76; ☑770 3113; www.bikecave.is; Einarsnes 36; ☺9am-11pm; ☐12) This unusual cafe (dishes kr900 to kr3000) caters to cyclists, with coffee, beer, wine, a shower, laundry and workshop for DIY repairs.

☆ Entertainment

★Húrra LIVE MUSIC
(Map p82; Tryggvagata 22; ☺5pm-1am Sun-Thu, to 4.30am Fri & Sat; ☎) Dark and raw, this large bar opens up its back room to make a concert venue, with live music or DJs most nights, and is one of the best places in town to close out the night. Run by the same folks as Bravó (Map p82; Laugavegur 22; ☺11am-1am Mon-Thu, to 3am Fri & Sat; ☎), it's got a range of beers on tap and happy hour runs till 9pm (beer or wine kr700).

★Bíó Paradís CINEMA
(Map p82; www.bioparadis.is; Hverfisgata 54; adult kr1600; ☎) This totally cool cinema, decked out in movie posters and vintage officeware, screens specially curated Icelandic films with English subtitles. It's a chance to see movies that you may not find elsewhere. Plus there's a happy hour from 5pm to 7.30pm.

Reykjavík City Theatre THEATRE, DANCE
(Borgarleikhúsið; Map p76; ☑568 8000; www.borgarleikhus.is; Listabraut 3, Kringlan; ☺closed

Jul & Aug) Stages plays and musicals, and is home to the Icelandic Dance Company (Map p76; ☑588 0900; www.id.is; Listabraut 3, Kringlan).

Laugardalsvöllur National Stadium STADIUM
(Map p76; ☑510 2914; Laugardalur) Iceland's football (soccer) passion is huge. Cup and international matches are played at this national stadium in Laugardalur. See the sports sections of Reykjavík's newspapers or Football Association of Iceland (Knattspyrnusamband Íslands – KSÍ; ☑510 2900; www.ksi.is), and buy tickets directly from the stadium.

Café Rosenberg LIVE MUSIC
(Map p82; ☑551 2442; Klapparstígur 25-27; ☺3pm-1am Mon-Thu, 4pm-3am Fri & Sat) This big, booklined shopfront is dotted with couches and cocktail tables, and hosts all manner of live acts, from local singer-songwriters to jazz groups, with broad-paned windows looking onto the street.

🔒 Shopping

Reykjavík's vibrant design culture makes for great shopping: from sleek fish-skin purses and *lopapeysur* (Icelandic woollen sweaters) to unique music or the Icelandic schnapps *brennivín*. Laugavegur is the most dense shopping street. You'll find interesting shops all over town, but fashion concentrates near the Frakkastígur and Vitastígur end of Laugavegur. Skólavörðustígur is strong for arts and jewellery, while Bankastræti and Austurstræti have touristy shops.

Don't forget – all visitors are eligible for a 15% tax refund on their shopping, under certain conditions.

★Álafoss CLOTHING
(☑566 6303; www.alafoss.is; Álafossvegur 23, Mosfellsbær; ☺9am-6pm Mon-Fri, to 4pm Sat; ☐15) One of the best places in Iceland for hand- or machine-made *lopapeysur* and other wool products, this factory-outlet in Mosfellsbær, one of Reykjavík's outer suburbs, can be an add-on to your Golden Circle or Ring Road adventure. Prices are somewhat lower than most tourist shops. Reykjavík bus 15 stops nearby (Háholt stop). Álafoss also has a Reykjavík boutique (Map p82; ☑562 6303; www.alafoss.is; Laugavegur 8; ☺10am-6pm).

★Kiosk CLOTHING
(Map p82; ☑445 3269; www.kioskreykjavik.com; Laugavegur 65; ☺11am-6pm Mon-Fri, to 5pm Sat) This wonderful designers' cooperative is lined with creative women's fashion in a

glass-fronted boutique. Designers take turns (wo)manning the store.

Kirsuberjatréð
ARTS & CRAFTS

(Cherry Tree; Map p82; ☑562 8990; www.kirs.is; Vesturgata 4; ☺10am-7pm & 8-10pm Mon-Fri, to 5pm Sat, to 4pm Sun) This women's art-and-design collective in an interesting 1882 former bookshop sells weird and wonderful fish-skin handbags, music boxes made from string, and, our favourite, beautiful coloured bowls made from radish slices. It's been around for 25 years and now has 11 designers.

Orrifinn
JEWELLERY

(Map p82; ☑789 7616; www.facebook.com/OrrifinnJewels/; Skólavörðustígur 17a; ☺10am-6pm Mon-Fri, to 4pm Sat) Subtle, beautiful jewellery captures the natural wonder of Iceland and its Viking history. Delicate anchors, axes and pen nibs dangle from understated matte chains.

Skúmaskot
ARTS & CRAFTS

(Map p82; ☑663 1013; www.facebook.com/skumaskot.art.design/; Skólavörðustígur 21a; ☺10am-6pm Mon-Fri, to 5pm Sat, noon-4pm Sun) Ten local designers create these unique handmade porcelain items, women's and kids' clothing, paintings and cards. It's in a recently renovated large gallery beautifully showcasing their creative Icelandic crafts.

Mál og Menning
BOOKS

(Map p82; ☑580 5000; www.bmm.is; Laugavegur 18; ☺9am-10pm Mon-Fri, 10am-10pm Sat; ☜) This popular and well-stocked independent bookshop carries great English-language books for getting under the skin of Iceland. Check out *Thermal Pools in Iceland* by Jón G Snæland and Þóra Sigurbjörnsdóttir; you can browse it in the lively cafe. Also sells CDs, games and newspapers.

Kraum
ARTS & CRAFTS

(Map p82; www.kraum.is; Bankastræti 7; ☺9am-7pm Mon-Fri, 10am-6pm Sat, 11am-6pm Sun) The brainchild of a band of local artists, Kraum literally means 'simmering', like the island's quaking earth and the inventive minds of its citizens. Expect a fascinating assortment of unique designer wares, like fish-skin apparel and driftwood furniture. Find it downstairs in the large Cintamani store.

Kolaportið Flea Market
MARKET

(Map p82; www.kolaportid.is; Tryggvagata 19; ☺11am-5pm Sat & Sun) Held in a huge industrial building by the harbour, this weekend market is a Reykjavík institution. There's a huge tumble of secondhand clothes and old toys, plus cheap imports. There's also a food section that sells traditional eats like *rúgbrauð* (geothermally baked rye bread), *brauðterta* ('sandwich cake', a layering of bread with mayonnaise-based fillings) and *hákarl* (fermented shark).

Farmers Market
CLOTHING

(Map p76; ☑552 1960; www.farmersmarket.is; Hólmaslóð 2; ☺10am-6pm Mon-Fri, 11am-4pm Sat, noon-4pm Sun) ✿ This design company run by a local couple is not about food, but rather sustainably designed and created clothing, accessories and housewares with an emphasis on natural fabrics and materials.

Kron
SHOES

(Map p82; ☑551 8388; www.kron.is; Laugavegur 48; ☺10am-6pm Mon-Thu, to 6.30pm Fri, to 5pm Sat) Kron sells its own outlandishly wonderful handmade shoes with all the flair you'd expect of an Icelandic label. Colours are bright, textures are cool, and they're even wearable (those practical Icelanders!).

12 Tónar
MUSIC

(Map p82; www.12tonar.is; Skolavörðustígur 15; ☺10am-6pm Mon-Sat, noon-6pm Sun) A very cool place to hang out, 12 Tónar is responsible for launching some of Iceland's favourite bands. In the two-storey shop you can listen to CDs, drink coffee and sometimes catch a live performance.

ℹ Information

Landspítali University Hospital (☑543 1000, doctor on duty ☑1770; www.landspitali.is; Fossvogur) Casualty department open 24/7.

Main Tourist Office (Upplýsingamiðstöð Ferðamanna; Map p82; ☑590 1550; www.visitreykjavik.is; Aðalstræti 2; ☺8am-8pm) Friendly staff and mountains of free brochures, plus maps, Reykjavík City Card and Strætó city bus tickets for sale. Books accommodation, tours and activities.

Reykjavík City Card (www.citycard.is; 24/48/72hr kr3500/4700/5500) The Reykjavík City Card offers admission to Reykjavík's municipal swimming/thermal pools and to most of the main galleries and museums, plus discounts on some tours, shops and entertainment. Also gives free travel on the city's Strætó buses and on the ferry to Viðey. The card is available at the Main Tourist Office, some travel agencies, 10-11 supermarkets, HI hostels and some hotels.

ⓘ TRANSPORT TO/FROM KEFLAVÍK INTERNATIONAL AIRPORT

The journey from Keflavík International Airport to Reykjavík takes about 50 minutes. Three easy bus services connect Reykjavík and the airport and are the best transport option; kids get discounted fares.

Airport Direct (📞 497 5000; www.reykjaviksightseeing.is/airport-direct; 🚌) Minibuses operated by Reykjavík Sightseeing shuttle between hotels and the airport (kr4500, return kr8000).

Airport Express (📞 540 1313; www.airportexpress.is; 🚌) Operated by Gray Line Tours between Keflavík International Airport and Lækjartorg Sq in central Reykjavík (kr2100) or Mjódd bus terminal, or via hotel pickup/drop off (kr2700; book ahead). Has connections to Borgarnes and points north, including Akureyri.

Flybus (📞 580 5400; www.re.is; 🚌) Operated by Reykjavík Excursions, Flybus meets all international flights. One-way tickets cost kr2200. Pay kr2800 for hotel pickup/drop off (which shuttles you from/to the Flybus at the BSÍ bus terminal); you must schedule hotel pickup a day ahead. A separate service runs to the Blue Lagoon (from where you can continue to the city centre or the airport; kr3900). Buy tickets online, at many hotels, or at the airport booth. Flybus will also drop off/pick up in Garðabær and Hafnarfjörður, just south of Reykjavík.

Strætó (www.bus.is) Bus 55 also connects the BSÍ bus terminal and the airport (kr1680, nine daily Monday to Friday in summer).

Taxis cost around kr15,000.

Visit Iceland (📞 511 4000; www.visiticeland.com; Borgartún 35) Vast Iceland-wide information.

ⓘ Getting There & Around

AIR

Keflavík International Airport (p124) Iceland's primary international airport, 48km west of Reykjavík, on the Reykjanes Peninsula.

Reykjavík Domestic Airport (p124) In central Reykjavík, just south of Tjörnin. Sightseeing services, domestic flights and those to/from Greenland and the Faeroe Islands fly here.

BICYCLE

Reykjavík has a steadily improving network of cycle lanes; ask the Main Tourist Office for a map. You are allowed to cycle on pavements as long as you don't cause pedestrians problems.

At the Old Harbour, rent bikes at **Reykjavík Bike Tours** (Reykjavík Segway Tours; Map p82; 🚲 bike 694 8956, segway 897 2790; www.icelandbike.com; Ægisgarður 7, Old Harbour; bike rental per 4hr from kr3500, tours from kr6500; ⏰ 9am-5pm Jun-Aug, reduced hours Sep-May; 🚌14) and get service at **Kría** (Map p76; www.kriacycles.com; Grandagarður 5; ⏰10am-6pm Mon-Fri, 11am-1pm Sat) bicycle shop, or do your own repairs at Bike Cave (p93) cafe.

BUS

The free *Public Transport in Iceland* map (www.publictransport.is) has a good overview of routes.

Strætó (www.bus.is) operates regular, easy-to-use buses around Reykjavík and its suburbs; it also operates long-distance buses. Buses run from 7am until 11pm or midnight daily (from 11am on Sunday). Services depart at 20-minute or 30-minute intervals. A limited night-bus service runs until 2am on Friday and Saturday.

The fare is kr420; you can buy tickets at the bus terminal, pay on board (though no change is given) or by using its app. Buy one-/three-day passes (kr1500/3500) at Mjódd bus terminal, the Main Tourist Office, 10-11 convenience stores and many hotels.

The Reykjavík City Card also acts as a Strætó bus pass.

TAXI

Taxi prices are high. Flagfall starts at around kr680. Tipping is not required. From BSÍ bus terminal to Harpa concert hall costs about kr2000. From Mjódd bus terminal it's about kr4100.

There are usually taxis outside bus stations, airports and bars on weekend nights (huge queues for the latter), plus on Bankastræti near Lækjargata.

BSR (📞 561 0000; www.taxireykjavik.is)
Hreyfill (📞 588 5522; www.hreyfill.is)

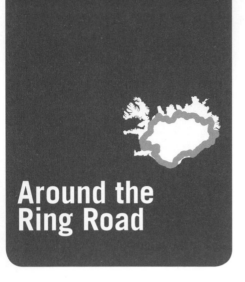

Around the Ring Road

The Golden Circle

The Golden Circle takes in three popular attractions all within 100km of the capital: Þingvellir, Geysir and Gullfoss. It is an artificial tourist circuit (ie no natural topography marks its extent) that is loved (and marketed) by thousands, and not to be confused with the Ring Road, which wraps around the entire country.

Þingvellir National Park (p26)

👁 Sights & Activities

Ljósafoss Power Station　　　MUSEUM
(Ljósafossstöð; 📞 896 7407; www.landsvirkjun. com; Ljósafoss; ⏰ 10am-5pm Jun-Aug, reduced hours Sep-May) **FREE** The 1937 Ljósafoss Power Station catches the outflow of lake Úlfljótsvatn and turns it into power. In 2016 an elaborate state-of-the-art multimedia exhibition called Powering the Future opened, bringing principles of electricity, hydropower, and geothermal and renewable energy to life. Free at the time of writing, a fee may be instituted; check the website for updates on opening hours and costs.

🛌 Sleeping

Þingvellir Campsites　　　CAMPGROUND €
(www.thingvellir.is; sites per adult/child/tent kr1300/free/100; ⏰ Jun-Sep) Overseen by the park information centre, the best two areas are at Leirar, near the cafe: Syðri-Leirar is the biggest and Nyrðri-Leirar has laundry facilities. Fagrabrekka and Hvannabrekka are for campers only (no cars). Vatnskot is down by the lake and has toilets and cold water (no electricity).

Lake Thingvellir Cottages　　　COTTAGES €€
(📞 892 7110; www.lakethingvellir.is; Heiðarás; cottages kr18,500, plus per person per night kr2400; 🅿🛜) Four modern pine cottages with views to the lake sit near the national-park entrance along Rte 36.

Ion Luxury Adventure Hotel　　　BOUTIQUE HOTEL €€€
(📞 482 3415; www.ioniceland.is; Nesjavellir vid Þingvallavatn; d kr50,100; 🅿♨🛜🏊) 🍴 A leader in a new breed of deluxe countryside hotels, Ion is all about hip, modern rooms and sustainable practices. Its geothermal pool, organic spa, restaurant with slow-food local ingredients and bar with floor-to-ceiling plate-glass windows are all sumptuous. Rooms are a tad smallish, but kitted out impeccably, with fun touches such as horse portraits on the walls.

Hótel Grimsborgir　　　HOTEL €€€
(📞 555 7878; www.grimsborgir.com; d incl breakfast kr49,200, 2-bedroom apt kr66,000; 🛜) Hótel Grimsborgir offers fully kitted-out luxury hotel suites and apartments. Find

it on Rte 36, 5.5km south of Ljósafossstöð, and 5km north of the junction with Rte 35.

✖ Eating

Silfra Restaurant ICELANDIC €€€
(www.ioniceland.is; Nesjavellir vid Þingvallavatn; mains lunch kr2500-6000, dinner kr5000-7000; ⊙11.30am-10pm) The restaurant at the Ion Luxury Adventure Hotel serves modern Icelandic fare with a slow-food twist, featuring locally sourced ingredients.

❶ Information

Þingvellir Information Centre (Leirar Þjónustumiðstöð; ☑482 2660; www.thing vellir.is; ⊙9am-8pm May-Sep, to 5pm Oct-Apr) On Rte 36, on the north side of the lake, the information centre has details about the national park, as well as a basic **cafe** (soup kr990; ⊙9am-10pm Apr-Oct, reduced hours Nov-Mar).

Þingvellir Visitors Centre (Gestastofa; ☑482 3613; ⊙9am-6.30pm Apr-Oct, to 5pm Nov-Mar) At the top of the Almannagjá rift is a simple visitors centre with a video on the area's nature and history, and a shop. The adjacent boardwalk offers great valley views. Toilets cost kr200. You can park here and walk down, or walk up from the Alþingi site.

Laugarvatn (p27)

🛏 Sleeping & Eating

Laugarvatn HI Hostel HOSTEL €
(☑486 1215; www.laugarvatnhostel.is; dm/s/d without bathroom kr4100/7000/10,900, s/d kr13,400/16,650; ℗@😊) This large hostel, spread over several buildings along the village's main street, is professional and comfortable. There's a newly renovated two-storey building with plenty of kitchen space (great lake views while washing up or from the dining room). Some buildings are much smaller and houselike. There's a kr700 discount for HI members.

★Héraðsskólinn HOSTEL, GUESTHOUSE €€
(☑537 8060; www.heradsskolinn.is; dm/s/d/q without bathroom from kr5400/14,000/15,300/30,100, d with bathroom kr25,400; ℗😊) This sparkling hostel and guesthouse fills an enormous renovated historical landmark school, built in 1928 by Guðjón Samúelsson. The beautiful lakeside building with peaked roofs offers both private rooms with shared bathrooms (some sleep up to six) and dorms, plus a spa-

WORTH A TRIP

HALLDÓR LAXNESS HOUSE

Nobel Prize–winning author Halldór Laxness (1902–98) lived in Mosfells-bær all his life. His riverside home is now the **Gljúfrasteinn Laxness Museum** (☑586 8066; www.gljufra steinn.is; Mosfellsbær; adult/child kr900/free; ⊙9am-5pm Jun-Aug, 10am-5pm Tue-Sun Mar-May, Sep, Oct & Dec, 10am-5pm Tue-Fri Jan, Feb & Nov), easy to visit on the road from Reykjavík to Þingvellir (Rte 36). The author built this upper-class 1950s house and it remains intact with original furniture, writing room and Laxness' fine-art collection (needlework, sweetly, by his wife Auður). An audio tour leads you round. Look for his beloved Jaguar parked out the front.

cious library/living room and a cafe (open 7.30am to 10pm).

★Efstidalur II GUESTHOUSE €€
(☑486 1186; www.efstidalur.is; Efstidalur 2, Bláskógabyggð; d/tr incl breakfast from kr26,200/29,700; ℗😊) Located 12km northeast of Laugarvatn on a working dairy farm, Efstidalur offers wonderfully welcoming digs, tasty meals and amazing ice cream. Adorable semidetached cottages have brilliant views of hulking Hekla, and the restaurant serves beef from the farm and trout from the lake. The ice-cream bar scoops farm ice cream (kr400 per scoop) and has windows looking into the dairy barn.

Geysir & Gullfoss (p28)

🛏 Sleeping

Gljasteinn Skálinn CABIN, GUESTHOUSE €
(☑486 8757; www.gljasteinn.is; Myrkholt; dm adult/child kr6500/4000, d without bathroom kr11,000) This beautiful farm in the widening sweep of the valley between Geysir and Gullfoss has a clutch of tidy houses, one of which has dorms and doubles with shared bathrooms, a kitchen and living room. A nearby three-bedroom cabin (from kr25,500) is a great bargain. It also has cabins with dorm beds in the highlands on the Kjölur route (F35).

Mengi GUESTHOUSE €€

(📞780 1414; www.mengi-kjarnholt.com; Kjarnholt; d/f without bathroom from kr18,400/25,000; P 📶) This freshly renovated farmhouse in the countryside 10km south of Geysir has 10 rooms with sweeping pastoral views and a shared geothermal hot tub.

Flúðir (p28)

🛏 Sleeping & Eating

**Grund –
Guesthouse Flúðir** GUESTHOUSE €€

(Gistiheimilið Flúðum; 📞565 9196; www.gisting fludir.is; d with/without bathroom incl breakfast kr25,000/20,000; P 📶) This adorable guesthouse has five homey rooms filled with antiques, and a new wing of rooms opened in 2016 with private bathrooms and decks with mountain views. The popular restaurant prides itself on offering fresh local food.

**★Minilik Ethiopian
Restaurant** ETHIOPIAN €€

(📞846 9798; www.minilik.is; mains kr2000-3000; ⊙noon-9pm Jun-Aug, 6-9pm Sep-May; 🍴) Azeb cooks up traditional Ethiopian specialities in this welcoming, unpretentious spot. There are loads of vegetarian options, but also lamb dishes such as *awaze tibs* or chicken *(doro kitfo)*. As far as we know, this is the only Ethiopian restaurant in Iceland, and it should beckon all lovers of spice.

Hvolsvöllur & Around (p30)

🛏 Sleeping

Asgarður COTTAGES €

(📞487 1440; www.asgardurinn.is; d without bathroom kr13,200; 📶) These cute picket-lined individual cottages cluster under a stand of trees. They have two bedrooms and private bathrooms and kitchenettes. A quaint restored 1927 schoolhouse sits in the centre. Made-up beds cost kr6600 and sleeping-bag accommodation is kr4900. Camping is also available.

Spói Guesthouse B&B €€

(📞861 8687; www.spoiguesthouse.is; Hlíðarvegur 15; d without bathroom kr17,000; P 📶) This impeccable family-run guesthouse has a collection of pristine rooms grouped around

a large dining room with a broad wooden table for the lavish breakfast. The owners offer a wealth of local knowledge.

🍴 Eating

★Eldstó Art Café CAFE €€

(📞482 1011; www.eldsto.is; Austurvegur 2, Hvolsvöllur; mains kr2000-4000; ⊙11am-9.30pm Jun-Aug; P 📶) Eldstó offers fresh-brewed coffee, homemade daily specials (such as coconut curry soup) and a couple of outdoor Ring Road–side tables. Friendly owners are ceramicists with a small on-site gallery, and also offer simple accommodation upstairs (doubles from kr28,000).

Skógar (p31)

🛏 Sleeping

★Skógar Campsite CAMPGROUND €

(sites per adult/child kr1200/800; ⊙May-Sep) Basic grassy lot with a great location, right by Skógafoss; the sound of falling water makes a soothing lullaby. There's a no-frills toilet block (shower kr300); pay at the hostel nearby.

Skógar HI Hostel HOSTEL €

(📞487 8780; www.hostel.is; dm/d kr4750/12,900; 📶) A solid link in the HI chain, this spot is located a stone's throw from Skógafoss in an old school with utilitarian rooms. There's a guest kitchen and a laundry.

★Skógar Guesthouse GUESTHOUSE €€

(📞894 5464; www.skogarguesthouse.is; d/tr without bathroom incl breakfast kr21,000/30,000; 📶) This charming white farmhouse is tucked back inside the trees, beyond the

Hótel Edda, almost to the cliff face. A friendly family offers quaint, impeccably maintained rooms with crisp linens and cosy quilts, a large, immaculate kitchen and bathrooms, and a hot tub on a wood deck beneath the maples. It feels well out of the tourist fray despite being in central Skógar.

Hótel Skógafoss   HOTEL €€

(☑ 487 8780; www.hotelskogafoss.is; d incl breakfast with/without waterfall view kr27,000/25,000; 🛜) This hotel opened in 2014 and offers simple, modern rooms (half of which have views of Skógafoss; ask when booking) with good bathrooms.

🍴 Eating

Hótel Skógafoss Bistro-Bar   ICELANDIC €€

(☑ 487 8780; www.hotelskogafoss.is; mains kr1600-2500; ⊙ 8am-11pm Jun-Sep, to 10pm Oct-May) The bistro-bar at Hótel Skógafoss is one of the best eating and drinking spots in town, with plate-glass windows looking onto the falls and local beer on tap.

Vík (p33)

🛏 Sleeping

★ Garðar   GUESTHOUSE €

(☑ 487 1260; www.reynisfjara-guesthouses.com; Reynisfjara; cottages kr12,000-18,000) Garðar, at the end of Rte 215, to the west of Vík, is a magical, view-blessed place. Friendly farmer Ragnar rents out self-contained beachside huts: one stone cottage sleeps four, other timber cottages sleep two to four. Note that linen costs kr1500 per person.

Vík HI Hostel   HOSTEL €

(Norður-Vík Hostel; ☑ 487 1106; www.hostel.is; Suðurvíkurvegur 5; dm/d without bathroom kr4750/12,900, cottages from kr32,800; @ 🛜) 🏷 Vík's small, homey, year-round hostel is found in the beige house on the hill behind the village centre. Good facilities include a guest kitchen and bike hire (per half-/full day kr2000/3000), plus several stand-alone cottages sleeping up to eight people. The staff can also arrange local tours (from kr9000) and paragliding (kr35,000; May to September). There's a kr750 discount for HI members. The hostel is green-certified.

★ Guesthouse Carina   B&B €€

(☑ 699 0961; www.guesthousecarina.is; Mýrarbraut 13; s/d/q without bathroom incl breakfast from kr16,900/21,900/31,500; P 🛜) Friendly Carina and her husband Ingvar run one of the best lodging options in Vík. Neat-as-a-pin, spacious rooms with good light and clean shared bathrooms fill a large converted house near the centre of town.

★ Grand Guesthouse Garðakot   B&B €€

(☑ 487 1441; www.ggg.is; Garðakot farm; d kr26,000; 🛜) Set on a pastoral sheep farm, this small, tidy house holds four beautiful rooms, two with private bathrooms and two which share. Heated hardwood floors downstairs, sweeping views of volcanoes and sea upstairs, and friendly proprietors, pretty decor, serenity and flat-screen TVs for all. It's 14km west of Vík, south of the Ring Road on Rte 218.

★ Icelandair Hótel Vík   HOTEL €€€

(☑ 487 1480, booking 444 4000; www.icelandairhotels.com; Klettsvegur 1-5; d/tr/f from kr24,500/29,000/50,000; P 🛜) This sleek black-window-fronted hotel is improbably tucked just behind the Hótel Edda, on the eastern edge of town, near the campground. The hotels share a lobby (and have the same friendly owners), but that's where the resemblance ends. The Icelandair hotel has suitably swanky rooms, some with views to the rear cliffs or the sea. The light, natural decor is inspired by the local environment.

DON'T MISS

FIMMVÖRÐUHÁLS TREK

Fimmvörðuháls – named for a pass between two brooding glaciers – dazzles the eye with a parade of wild inland vistas. Linking **Skógar** and **Þórsmörk**, the awesome hike is 23.4km long, and can be divided into three distinct sections of somewhat equal length. Figure around 10 hours to complete the trek, which includes stops to rest, and to check out the steaming remnants of the Eyjafjallajökull eruption. It's best to tackle the hike from July to mid-September. Pack wisely; you can experience all four seasons over the course of this hike. If in doubt, go with a guide, as there are two treacherous passes, and tours here are great.

✖ Eating

★ Suður-Vík ICELANDIC, ASIAN €€
(✔ 487 1515; www.facebook.com/Sudurvik; Suður-víkurvegur 1; mains kr2100-5000; ⊙ noon-10pm)
The friendly ambience, from hardwood floors and interesting artwork to smiling staff, helps elevate this restaurant beyond the competition. Food is Icelandic hearty, and ranges from heaping steak sandwiches with bacon and Béarnaise sauce to Asian (think Thai satay with rice). In a warmly lit silver building atop town. Book ahead in summer.

Svarta Fjaran CAFE €€
(Black Beach Restaurant; ✔ 571 2718; www.svarta fjaran.com; Reynisfjara; snacks kr990, dinner mains kr2500-6000; ⊙ 11am-10pm; 🛜)
Black volcanic cubes, meant to mimic the nearby black beach Reynisfjara with its famous basalt columns, house this contemporary restaurant that serves homemade cakes and snacks during the day and a full dinner menu at night. Plate-glass windows give views to the ocean and Dyrhólaey beyond.

ℹ Information

Tourist Information Centre (✔ 487 1395; www.visitvik.is; Víkurbraut 28; ⊙ 10am-8pm Mon-Fri, 11am-5pm Sat & Sun Jun-Aug; 🛜) Inside the Brydebúð museum on the west side of the village.

Kirkjubæjarklaustur (p37)

☞ Tours

Kind Adventure MOUNTAIN BIKING
(✔ 847 1604; www.kindadventure.is) This new company is run by a young farming couple (*kind* means sheep) who are passionate about their surrounds. Tours are on fatbikes (off-road bicycles with oversized tyres) that are perfect for the Icelandic conditions (snow, mud, sand) and enable year-round tours (two to three hours for kr15,500). There's also a two-day adventure to the Laki craters (kr130,000).

🛏 Sleeping

Kirkjubær II CAMPGROUND €
(✔ 894 4495; www.kirkjubaer.com; sites per person kr1300, cottages kr18,000; ⊙ camping Jun-Sep, cottages Apr-Oct) Neat green site with sheltering hedges, right in town. Good service buildings include kitchen, showers and laundry. A boon in bad weather: a half-dozen basic huts, each sleeping four in bunk beds (BYO sleeping bag).

Hörgsland CAMPGROUND, COTTAGES €€
(✔ 487 6655; www.horgsland.is; sites per person kr1250, cottages for 2/6 from kr19,200/35,400, d with/without bathroom incl breakfast kr22,300/18,800; 🛜) On the Ring Road about 8km northeast of Klaustur is this mini village of 13 spotless, spacious, self-contained cottages that can sleep six (note: on the website, these cottages are called 'guesthouses'). A recent addition is a block of spick-and-span rooms, with and without bathroom. There's also camping, plus outdoor hot-pots, and a simple shop and cafe serving breakfast and dinner.

ℹ Information

Skaftárstofa Visitor Centre (✔ 487 4620; www.visitklaustur.is; Klausturvegur 2; ⊙ 9am-6pm mid-Apr–mid-Oct) The helpful tourist office is located inside the Skaftárstofa Visitor Centre, with good local information plus coverage and exhibitions on Katla Geopark and Vatnajökull National Park – this is the base

---

ℹ RESPECTING NATURE

Tantalising as the sights of Iceland may be, with its black-sand beaches and glaciers glinting along the roadside, it is paramount to realise that there are real dangers involved. For example, the famous beach Reynisfjara (p33) near Vík is known for rogue waves, and tourists are regularly rescued or drowned there. As for glaciers, no one should go onto them without experienced, local guidance. Crevasses form suddenly and are often invisible (beneath snow), gasses can be emitted by volcanic activity, and flooding (sometimes invisible from above) can destabilise the ice even further.

With the growing popularity of tourism in Iceland, the foolhardy behaviour of inexperienced visitors regularly makes the news (one man drove his family onto a glacier in a rental car). Don't be one of them. Always check on local conditions, change your plan if it's not safe, and log your treks with www.safetravel.is.

Turf-roofed church in Hof, Skaftafell

for the lesser-visited western pocket of the national park, best accessed from the Fjallabak route (Rte F208), and only accessible by 4WD or bus. There's also a short film on the Laki eruption.

Lómagnúpur & Around (p37)

🛏 Sleeping

⭐**Dalshöfði Guesthouse**   GUESTHOUSE €€
(☑ 861 4781; dalshofdi@gmail.com; s/d without bathroom incl breakfast kr13,000/18,300; ⊙ Mar-Oct) An appealing option in this area is Dalshöfði Guesthouse, in a remote and scenic farm setting 5km north of the Ring Road. Rooms are bright and spotless, with access to a kitchen and a sunny, plant-filled outdoor deck. There's a two-bedroom apartment (kr33,200) here too, and some lovely hiking trails in the area.

Skaftafell (p38)

☞ Tours

Atlantsflug   SCENIC FLIGHT
(☑ 854 4105; www.flightseeing.is) Sightseeing flights offer a brilliant perspective over all this natural splendour, and leave from the tiny airfield on the Ring Road, just by the turn-off to the Skaftafellsstofa Visitor Centre. Choose between six tour options, with views over Landmannalaugar, Lak-agígar, Skaftafell peaks, Jökulsárlón and Grímsvötn. Prices start from kr26,100 for 20 minutes on the 'pilot special' surprise route (determined by weather and conditions).

Glacier Guides   ADVENTURE TOUR
(☑ Reykjavík 562 7000, Skaftafell 659 7000; www.glacierguides.is; ⊙ 8.30am-6pm Apr-Oct, reduced hours Nov-Mar) As well as glacier walks of varying duration and difficulty, Glacier Guides also offers ice climbing, plus wintertime ice-cave visits from Skaftafell. Its beginner-level walk is the family-friendly 'Glacier Wonders', a 3½-hour tour with a one-hour walk on Falljökull (adult/child kr10,990/5495, minimum age 10 years); trips depart from Skaftafell four times daily April to October.

Icelandic Mountain Guides   ADVENTURE TOUR
(IMG; ☑ Reykjavík 587 9999, Skaftafell 894 2959; www.mountainguides.is;   ⊙ 8.30am-6pm May-Sep, reduced hours Oct-Apr) IMG's best-selling walk is the family-friendly 'Blue Ice Experience', with 1½ to two hours spent on the ice at Svínafellsjökull (adult/child kr10,900/5450, minimum age eight years). They run from Skaftafell two to six times daily year-round (departures at 10am and

2pm year-round, plus additional tours from June to September).

Local Guide
ADVENTURE TOUR

(☑ 894 1317; www.localguide.is; Fagurhólsmýri; ⊙ 9am-5pm) Local Guide's booking agency is at Fagurhólsmýri (there's an N1 fuel pump there), about 26km from Skaftafell. From here, guides run tailored, year-round glacier hikes and ice climbs (the shortest tour offers 1½ hours on the ice for kr11,900). Local Guide is also the long-standing local expert on ice caves, running tours from mid-November to March.

🛏 Sleeping

Skaftafell Campsite
CAMPGROUND €

(☑ 470 8300; www.vjp.is; sites per adult/teen/child kr1600/750/free; ⊙ May-Sep; 🛜) Most visitors bring a tent (or campervan) to this large, gravelly, panoramic campsite (with laundry facilities, and hot showers for kr500). It gets very busy in summer, with a capacity of 400 pitches. Reservations are only required for large groups (40-plus people). No cooking facilities are provided. Wi-fi is available in the visitor centre.

ℹ Information

Skaftafellsstofa Visitor Centre (☑ 470 8300; www.vjp.is; ⊙ 9am-7pm May-Sep, 10am-5pm Feb-Apr, Oct & Nov, 11am-5pm Dec, 10am-4pm Jan; 🛜) The helpful year-round visitor centre has an information desk plus maps for sale, informative exhibitions, a summertime cafe and internet access. The staff here know their stuff.

Ingólfshöfði (p39)

🛏 Sleeping

Fosshotel Glacier Lagoon
HOTEL €€€

(☑ 514 8300; www.fosshotel.is; Hnappavellir; r incl breakfast from kr33,600; 🛜) The name is misleading: this large new four-star hotel sits halfway between Skaftafell and Jökulsárlón at Hnappavellir, about 3km east of the departure point for Ingólfshöfði tours. There are *no* lagoon views – Jökulsárlón is a 20-minute drive away. Opened in mid-2016, the newly constructed hotel houses 104 simple but stylish rooms, a good restaurant and an inviting bar area.

Around Jökulsárlón (p40)

🏃 Activities

Breiðármörk Trail
WALKING

A new walking trail has been marked from the western car park at Jökulsárlón, leading to Breiðárlón (10km one way) and Fjallsárlón (15.3km) lagoons. It is classified as challenging. In time, there is a plan to build out this walking route from Skaftafell in the west to Lónsöræfi in the east.

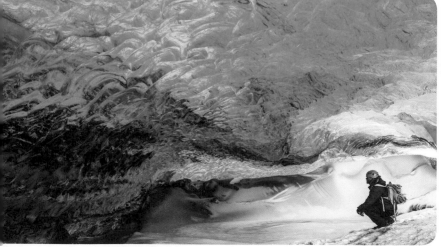

Ice cave in Vatnajökull National Park (p40)

The visitor centre at Höfn sells a trail map (kr250).

Hali to Höfn

🏃 Tours

Glacier Adventure　　　ADVENTURE TOUR
(📞 571 4577; www.glacieradventures.is; Hali) The closest guiding company to Jökulsárlón, locally owned Glacier Adventure operates out of the **Hali Country Hotel** (📞 478 1073; www.hali.is; s/d/apt incl breakfast kr28,500/36,500/55,300; 🛜), about 13km east of the lagoon. Glacier walks are done on Breiðamerkurjökull, with one to 1½ hours on the ice (adult/child kr15,500/8000). Half-day ice-climbing excursions (kr21,900), and winter ice-cave visits (from kr19,500), including a challenging option to a more remote cave, are also available.

🛏 Sleeping

⭐**Árnanes Country Lodge**　　　HOTEL €€
(📞 478 1550; www.arnanes.is; d with/without bathroom incl breakfast kr29,900/23,700; ⊗ Mar-Oct; 🛜) This polished, rural 18-room locale is 6km from Höfn and has motel units and guesthouse rooms. There's an agreeable summertime restaurant (mains kr2600 to kr6900) showcasing produce from neighbouring farms, and horse-riding tours for all skill levels (open to nonguests).

⭐**Skyrhúsid Guesthouse**　　　GUESTHOUSE €€
(📞 899 8384; www.facebook.com/skyrhusid; Hali; d/tr without bathroom incl breakfast kr19,000/23,000; 🛜) This cute, petite guesthouse is in Hali, right by Þórbergssetur. It's a cosy place with just nine fresh rooms (limited kitchen facilities), and a tiny, colourful breakfast area.

🍴 Eating

⭐**Jón Ríki**　　　ICELANDIC €€
(📞 478 2063; www.jonriki.is; Hólmur; mains lunch kr1390-2590, dinner kr2390-6490; ⊗ 11.30am-2pm Jun-late Aug, 6-9.30pm year-round) This fabulous farmhouse restaurant at Hólmur is something of a surprise, with funky decor, a small in-house brewery, and beautifully presented, high-quality dishes starring local produce: grilled langoustine, slow-roasted pork belly, white chocolate *skyr* for dessert. Sandwiches and soups

feature at lunchtime; pizza is also on the dinner menu. It can get busy, so a dinner reservation is advised.

Jöklasel Restaurant　　　ICELANDIC €€
(lunch buffet kr2500; ⊗ 11am-2pm Jul & Aug) Jöklasel, the base hut for Glacier Jeeps, is situated at the top of Rte F985, 840m above sea level. The restaurant at Jöklasel must have the most epic views in Iceland – it's like being on top of the world. There's coffee and snacks, plus a soup buffet at lunchtime.

Höfn (p43)

🎉 Festivals & Events

Humarhátíð　　　FOOD & DRINK
Every year in late June or early July, Höfn's annual langoustine festival honours this tasty crustacean, hauled to shore in abundance by the local fishing fleet. There's usually a fun fair, dancing, music, lots of alcohol and even a few langoustines.

🛏 Sleeping

Höfn Camping & Cottages　　　CAMPGROUND €
(📞 478 1606; www.campsite.is; Hafnarbraut 52; campsites per person kr1500, cottage d/q kr15,000/22,000; ⊗ Apr-Oct; @ 🛜) Lots of travellers stay at the campsite on the main road into town, where helpful owners and plenty of local info are among the draws. There are 11 good-value cottages, sleeping up to six; some have private toilet, but all use the amenities block for showers. There's also a playground and laundry, and some camping gear is sold at the reception.

⭐**Guesthouse Dyngja**　　　GUESTHOUSE €€
(📞 846 0161; www.dyngja.com; Hafnarbraut 1; d without bathroom incl breakfast kr19,300; @ 🛜) A lovely young couple own this petite five-room guesthouse in a prime harbourfront locale, and they have filled it with charm and good cheer: rich colours, a record player and vinyl selection, a self-service breakfast, an outdoor deck and good local knowledge. There's also a good new addition: a downstairs suite with private bathroom (kr23,200).

⭐**Milk Factory**　　　GUESTHOUSE €€
(📞 478 8900; www.milkfactory.is; Dalbraut 2; d/q incl breakfast kr24,600/31,750; 🛜) Full credit to the family – and the designers – behind

the masterful restoration of an old dairy factory north of town. Seventeen modern, hotel-standard rooms are here, including two with disabled access. The prize allotments are the six spacious mezzanine suites that sleep four – good for families or friends, although they don't have kitchens. There are also free bikes for guest use.

✖ Eating

Hafnarbúðin FAST FOOD €
(Ránarslóð; snacks & meals kr400-2600; ⊙ 9am-10pm Mon-Fri, 10am-10pm Sat & Sun) A fabulous relic, this tiny old-school diner has a cheap-and-cheerful vibe, a menu of fast-food favourites (hot dogs, burgers, toasted sandwiches) and a fine *humarloka* – langoustine baguette – for kr2000. There's even a drive-up window!

Djúpivogur (p47)

🛏 Sleeping

Hótel Framtíð HOTEL €€€
(☑ 478 8887; www.hotelframtid.com; Vogaland 4; s/d/apt from kr24,200/30,900/37,800; 🛜) This friendly hotel by the harbour is impressive for a village of this size. It's been around for a while (the original building was brought in pieces from Copenhagen in 1906), and there's an assortment of beds (and budgets) in various buildings. The hotel includes timber-lined hotel rooms, four cute cottages and five apartments (including two sleek, modern options).

There's also a building of rooms with shared bathroom (single/double kr17,900/21,000), and a more budget-friendly hostel (sleeping bag single/double kr7600/12,100).

ℹ Information

Tourist Information Centre (☑ 470 8740; Bakki 3; ⊙ 9am-5pm Mon-Fri, 10am-4pm Sat & Sun mid-May–mid-Sep) The information centre is across from Bakkabuð craft store in the centre of the village.

Berufjörður (p47)

◎ Sights

Teigarhorn NATURE RESERVE
(www.teigarhorn.is; ⊙ 9am-5pm Jun-Aug) Rock-hounds will love the display of zeolites at this farm, now a natural monument and na-

ture reserve 5km northwest of Djúpivogur. It's renowned for its zeolite crystals, and the free **museum** is open from 1pm to 3pm. The farm has also developed lovely short walking trails around its coast, good for a leg-stretch and birdwatching.

Breiðdalsvík (p48)

🛏 Sleeping

Campsite CAMPGROUND €
(site per person kr1000; ⊙ Jun-Sep) Campers will find a small campsite behind Hótel Bláfell.

Hótel Bláfell HOTEL €€
(☑ 475 6770; www.hotelblafell.is; Sólvellir 14; s/d incl breakfast kr23,850/27,800; 🛜) Located in the centre of 'town' (we use that term lightly), Hótel Bláfell has smart monochrome rooms (some timber-lined), a sauna and a superb guest lounge with open fire. Don't be put off by the featureless decor of the restaurant – the evening buffet (kr5900) is justifiably popular, plus there are à la carte options, including pizza (mains kr1500 to kr4100).

Breiðdalur (p50)

🛏 Sleeping

★ Silfurberg GUESTHOUSE €€€
(☑ 475 1515; www.silfurberg.com; Þorgrímsstaðir; d incl breakfast from kr37,500; ⊙ Jun–mid-Sep; 🛜) Silfurberg is a stunning boutique guesthouse on a rural property about 50km south of Egilsstaðir (30km from Breiðdalsvík). Style, humour and craftsmanship have been used to convert a barn into first-class accommodation, containing four rooms, one suite, and delightful, deluxe common areas. The outdoor sauna and dome-enclosed hot-pot are icing on the cake. Meals by arrangement.

Egilsstaðir & Around (p51)

◎ Sights

Snæfellsstofa – National Park Visitor Centre VISITOR CENTRE
(☑ 470 0840; www.vjp.is; ⊙ 9am-5pm Jun-Aug, 10am-5pm May & Sep) FREE This stylish centre covers the eastern territory of the behemoth

that is Vatnajökull National Park. Excellent displays highlight the nature of Snæfell mountain and the eastern highlands, and staff sell maps and offer advice to travellers wishing to hike or otherwise experience the park.

Tours

Jeep Tours
JEEP TOUR

(898 2798; www.jeeptours.is) Knowledgeable Agnar runs excellent 4WD day tours from Egilsstaðir into the highlands: to Askja and Herðubreið (kr44,500), to Snæfell (kr39,500), or on reindeer-spotting safaris. This is also one of few companies visiting Kverkfjöll as a day tour (kr44,500), travelling via (sealed) Rte 910 to Kárahnjúkar dam before tackling remote 4WD tracks. Winter tours are available; check the website.

Sleeping

Olga Guesthouse
GUESTHOUSE €€

(860 2999; www.gistihusolgu.com; Tjarnabraut 3; d with/without bathroom incl breakfast kr24,990/20,990;) In a good central location, dressed-in-red Olga offers five rooms that share three bathrooms and a small kitchen – all the rooms come with tea- and coffee-making facilities, TV and fridge. Two doors down is Olga's sister, yellow

Birta Guesthouse, under the same friendly ownership and with similar high-quality facilities. Both of the guesthouses have an additional annexe containing en suite rooms.

Hótel Eyvindará
HOTEL, COTTAGES €€

(471 1200; www.eyvindara.is; Eyvindará II; s/d incl breakfast kr23,000/28,500; Apr-Oct;) Set 4km out of town (on Rte 94), Eyvindará is a handsome, family-run collection of new hotel rooms, plus some good motel-style units and timber cottages. The cottages sit hidden among fir trees, while motel rooms enjoy verandahs and views. There's a decent restaurant too (open mid-May to mid-September), and an inviting lounge area.

Gistihúsið – Lake Hotel Egilsstaðir
HOTEL €€€

(471 1114; www.lakehotel.is; r incl breakfast kr33,100;) The town was named after this farm and splendid heritage guesthouse (now big enough to warrant the 'hotel' label) on the banks of Lagarfljót, 300m west of the crossroads. In its old wing, en suite rooms retain a sense of character. In contrast, a new extension houses 30 modern, slightly anonymous hotel rooms. The Baðhúsið spa (471 1114; hotel guest/nonguest kr2000/3500; 10am-10pm) is on site.

Egilsstaðir

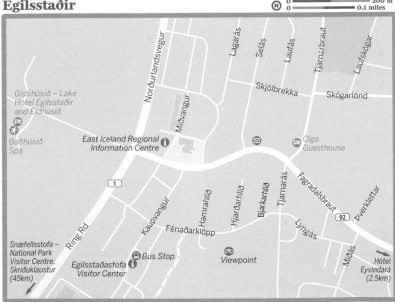

Eating

★ Klausturkaffi CAFE €€
(www.skriduklaustur.is; lunch buffet adult/child kr2990/1495; ⏲10am-6pm Jun-Aug, noon-5pm May & Sep; 👪) Klausturkaffi, inside the Skriðuklaustur museum (p51), serves an impeccable lunch buffet showcasing local ingredients (seafood soup, reindeer pie, brambleberry *skyr* cake). More tantalising, however, is every sweet-tooth's dream: the brilliant all-you-can-eat cake buffet (adult/child kr1990/995), served from 3pm.

Note that you don't have to pay to enter Skriðuklaustur if you are visiting the cafe.

★ Eldhúsið ICELANDIC €€€
(☎471 1114; www.lakehotel.is; lunch kr1390-3990, dinner mains kr3190-6190; ⏲11.30am-10pm; 📶) Some of the East's most creative cooking happens at the restaurant inside Gistihúsið – Lake Hotel Egilsstaðir (p105). The menu is an ode to locally sourced produce (lamb, fish, game), and the speciality is the beef, raised right here on the farm. Try a ribeye with Béarnaise foam, or 'surf and turf' tenderloin with tempura langoustine. Desserts are pretty, polished affairs. Bookings advised.

The three-course menu of farm produce costs kr8990 and represents good value for the high standard offered.

Information

East Iceland Regional Information Centre (☎471 2320; www.east.is; Miðvangur 1-3; ⏲8.30am-6pm Mon-Fri, 10am-4pm Sat, 1-6pm Sun Jun-Aug, 1-6pm Mon-Fri, 10am-2pm Sat Sep-May; 📶) Maps and brochures are plentiful here – you'll find everything you need to explore the entire eastern region. It shares the space with an excellent art and design store.

Víti crater
ANDREJ SEVKOVSKIJ/SHUTTERSTOCK ©

Egilsstaðastofa Visitor Center (☎470 0750; www.visitegilsstadir.is; Kaupvangur 17; ⏲7am-11pm Jun-Aug, 8.30am-3pm Mon-Fri May & Sep, 8.30am-12.30pm Mon-Fri Oct-Apr; 📶) From its info desk at the campground reception, this place focuses on Egilsstaðir and surrounds and can hook you up with bus tickets and various activity tours: hiking, super-Jeep tours, sea-angling etc. Bike hire is available (kr2900 for up to four hours, kr3900 for 24 hours).

Möðrudalur (p54)

Tours

Volcano Heli SCENIC FLIGHT
(☎647 3300; www.volcanoheli.is) Liechtenstein-born heli-pilot Matthias works from a summer base on Möðrudalur farm, and has epic highland landscapes in his backyard: Askja, Holuhraun, Mývatn and Kverkfjöll are all within a short flying time. The helicopter can carry three passengers, and rates are given for the entire trip (not per person). Prices start at kr106,200 for 30 minutes.

Mývatn & Around (p57)

Mývatn lake is circled by a 36km sealed road. The main settlement is **Reykjahlíð**, in the northeast corner – an information centre is here, as are most sleeping and eating options.

Sights

Víti GEOLOGICAL FORMATION
The dirt-brown crater of Víti reveals a secret when you reach its rim – a green pool of floodwater at its heart. The 300m-wide explosion crater was created in 1724 at the beginning of the destructive Mývatn Fires. There is a circular path around the rim of Víti to the geothermal area to its east.

Krafla Power Station POWER STATION
(⏲visitor centre 10am-5pm Jun-Aug) The idea of constructing a geothermal power station at Krafla was conceived in 1973, and preliminary work commenced with the drilling of holes to determine project feasibility. In 1975, however, after a long rest period, the Krafla fissure burst into activity. The project went ahead regardless and has been expand-

Mývatn & Krafla

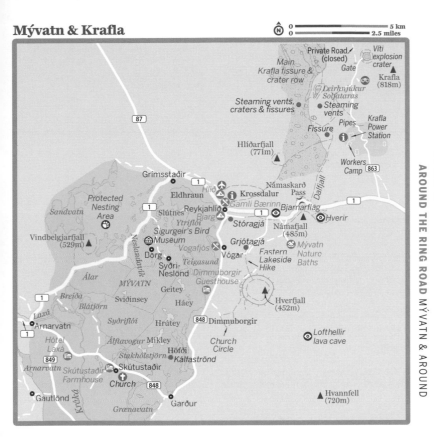

ed since. The power plant's visitor centre explains how it all works.

The **viewpoint** over the area (continue up Rte 863 to reach it) is impressive.

★ Lofthellir
CAVE

The dramatic lava cave at Lofthellir is a stunning destination, with magnificent natural ice sculptures (ice trolls?) dominating the interior.

Although it's one of Mývatn's highlights, the cave is on private property and can only be accessed on a half-day tour run by Saga Travel (p108). The tour involves a 45-minute 4WD journey and a 20-minute walk across a lava field to reach the cave itself, and then special equipment (headlamps, studded boots etc) and some wriggling through tight spaces. Dress warmly.

Vindbelgjarfjall
MOUNTAIN

The steep but relatively easy climb up 529m-high Vindbelgjarfjall (also known

as Vindbelgur), on Mývatn lake's western shore, offers one of the best views across the lake and its alien pseudocraters. The trail to the summit starts south of the peak, near the farm Vagnbrekka. Reckon on about a half-hour to reach the mount, and another half-hour to climb to the summit.

🏃 Activities & Tours

Geo Travel
ADVENTURE TOUR

(☑ 464 4442; www.geotravel.is) A small company owned by well-connected local guys. They work with the local operators to offer year-round tours, such as summer super-Jeep excursions to Askja and Holuhraun (kr38,000), Northern Lights tours (kr19,500), and winter hikes around Krafla (kr20,000).

Mývatn Activity – Hike&Bike
ADVENTURE TOUR

(☑ 899 4845; www.hikeandbike.is; ⊘ 9am-5pm Jun-Aug) Hike&Bike has a booth by the Gamli

ℹ MIDGES

Mývatn's name translates as 'lake of midges', and plaguelike swarms of these small flies are a lasting memory for many summer visitors. As infuriating as they can be, these midges are a vital food source for wildlife. If they bother you, consider wearing a head net (from the supermarket in Reykjahlíð, and elsewhere) – then splash on the repellent and pray for a good wind to send the little blighters diving.

Bærinn tavern in Reykjahlíð, offering tour bookings and mountain-bike rental (per day kr4500).

There's a summer program of cycling and hiking tours, including a four-hour walk to Hverfell and Dimmuborgir (p58; kr12,500); a three-hour pedal through the backcountry (kr12,500); and an evening sightseeing cycle that ends with a soak at the Mývatn Nature Baths (p57; kr12,500, including admission).

Saga Travel　　　　　ADVENTURE TOUR
(☑ 558 8888; www.sagatravel.is) Saga Travel operates an array of fabulous year-round tours in the Mývatn area, including sightseeing, caving, birdwatching and lava walks (see the website for the full selection). Its Northern Lights tours offer photography tips. There is often the option of joining tours from Akureyri or Reykjahlíð.

Snowdogs　　　　　DOG SLEDDING
(☑ 847 7199; www.snowdogs.is; tour adult/child kr30,000/15,000; ☺ Nov-Apr/May) On the remote farm Heiði, about 8km off the main road in southern Mývatn (take Rte 849 west of Skútustaðir), Sæmi and his family run dog-sledding tours across the snow-white wilderness. Tours vary depending on the dogs, people, weather and trail conditions, but guests are generally on the snow for about 45 to 60 minutes, and cover around 8km.

🛏 Sleeping

Mývatn's popularity means that room rates have soared; demand is far greater than supply, so be sure to book ahead. Most prices are very inflated, with €275 being the norm for a run-of-the-mill hotel double in summer's peak. Off-season rates are con-

siderably cheaper. To save money at guesthouses, ask about sleeping-bag options.

Most places are located either in Reykjahlíð or at Vógar, on the lake's eastern shore, with additional options at Dimmuborgir and Skútustaðir.

Bjarg　　　　　CAMPGROUND €
(☑ 464 4240; ferdabjarg@simnet.is; site per person kr1600, d without bathroom kr15,900; ☺ mid-May–Sep) This campsite has a gorgeous, peaceful location on the Reykjahlíð lakeshore – almost opposite the **supermarket** (☺ 9am-10pm mid-Jun–Aug, 10am-6pm Sep–mid-Jun) – and features a kitchen tent, laundry service, tour-booking desk, summer rowboat rental and bike hire. Accommodation is also available in a couple of rooms in the main building. Note: no wi-fi.

Hlíð　　　CAMPGROUND, GUESTHOUSE €
(☑ 464 4103; www.myvatnaccommodation.is; Hraunbrún; sites per person kr1600, dm kr5000, d incl breakfast kr25,000, cottage kr36,500; @ 🛜) Sprawling, well-run Hlíð is 300m uphill from the church and offers a full spectrum: camping, sleeping-bag dorms and rooms with kitchen access, no-frills huts, self-contained cottages sleeping six, and en suite guesthouse rooms. There's also a laundry, playground and bike hire.

★**Dimmuborgir Guesthouse**　　　GUESTHOUSE €€
(☑ 464 4210; www.dimmuborgir.is; d/cottages incl breakfast from kr22,100/28,500; 🛜) This lakeside complex close to Dimmuborgir (p58) lava field has a block of simple en suite rooms (with shared kitchen-dining area), plus a smattering of timber cottages, which range in size and include modern, well-equipped, family-sized options. Breakfast is served in the main house behind big picture windows overlooking the lake.

Skútustaðir Farmhouse　　　GUESTHOUSE €€
(☑ 464 4212; www.skutustadir.is; Skútustaðir; d with/without bathroom incl breakfast kr27,000/21,000; ☺ closed Christmas-New Year; 🛜) Slightly more accessible prices (in comparison to other options in the area), friendly owners and spotless facilities can be found at this recommended year-round guesthouse. Rooms in the homey farmhouse share bathroom, but there's also an annexe of five en suite rooms, plus a two-bedroom cottage, and a new block of rooms and large guest kitchen.

Icelandic horse

Hótel Laxá HOTEL €€€
(☑464 1900; www.hotellaxa.is; s/d incl breakfast kr32,800/39,400; 🛜) Bringing a breath of fresh air to Mývatn is this architecturally arresting, sustainably designed hotel, which opened in mid-2014 about 2km east of Skútustaðir. There are 80 modern, simple rooms – pricey but comfy, with colour schemes complementing the surrounds. The big windows and green sofas of the bar-lounge area invite contemplation; there's also a stylish on-site restaurant.

🍴 Eating

★ Vogafjós ICELANDIC €€
(☑464 3800; www.vogafjos.net; mains kr2500-5400; ⊙10am-11pm Jun-Aug, reduced hours Sep-May; 🛜☑🏠) The 'Cowshed', 2.5km south of Reykjahlíð, is a memorable restaurant where you can enjoy views of the lush surrounds, or of the dairy shed of this working farm (cows are milked at 7.30am and 5.30pm). The menu is an ode to local produce: smoked lamb, house-made mozzarella, dill-cured Arctic char, geysir bread, home-baked cakes, homemade ice cream.
Kitchen closes at 10pm in summer.

Gamli Bærinn ICELANDIC €€
(☑464 4270; www.myvatnhotel.is; snacks & mains kr950-3950; ⊙10am-11pm) The cheerfully busy 'Old Farm' tavern beside **Hótel Reynihlíð** (☑464 4170; www.myvatnhotel.is; s/d incl breakfast from kr28,800/34,400; @🛜) serves up good-quality pub-style meals all day, ranging from lamb soup to quiche to chicken salad and a pretty great salmon burger with potato salad. In the evening it becomes a local hang-out – the opening hours may be extended during weekend revelry, but the kitchen closes at 10pm.

ℹ️ Information

Mývatnsstofa Visitor Centre (☑464 4390; www.visitmyvatn.is; Hraunvegur 8, Reykjahlíð; ⊙7.30am-6pm Jun-Aug, reduced hours Sep-May) Located next to the supermarket in Reykjahlíð, this informative centre has displays on local geology, and can assist in booking accommodation, tours and transport. They also stock copies of the very useful *Mývatn* brochure, which provides an overview of hiking trails in the area.

Akureyri (p60)

🏃 Activities & Tours

★ Skjaldarvík HORSE RIDING, ADVENTURE TOUR
(☑552 5200; www.skjaldarvik.is; horse ride kr10,900, buggy tour kr19,900) As well as a superb guesthouse (p111) and restaurant, Skjaldarvík offers a couple of top-notch activities from its scenic fjordside locale 6km north of town: horse-riding tours, plus a fun new adrenaline option of buggy rides. These buggies are golf carts on steroids and seat two, and you drive along trails on

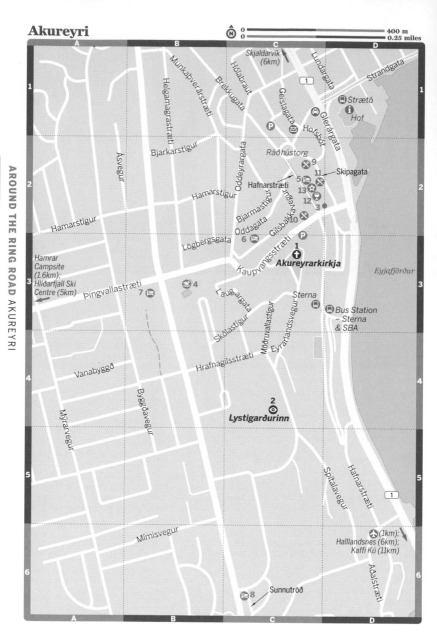

the surrounding farm (driver's licence required; helmet and overalls supplied).

Hlíðarfjall Ski Centre SKIING
(☎ 462 2280; www.hlidarfjall.is; day pass adult/child kr4900/1400; ♿) Iceland's premier

downhill ski slope is 5km west of town. The resort has a vertical drop of 455m; the longest trail is over 2.5km. There are seven lifts and 23 alpine slopes; there are also cross-country ski routes.

Akureyri

The season usually runs between December and late April, with the best conditions in February and March (Easter is particularly busy).

⭐ Festivals & Events

Iceland Winter Games   SPORTS
(www.icelandwintergames.com; ⊙ Mar) In March snowy activities take centre stage in Iceland's winter-sports capital, including international freeski and snowboard competitions. Tour operators offer ways to get out into gloriously wintry landscapes (like dog sledding, snowmobiling, and super-Jeep or helicopter tours). Rug up!

🛏 Sleeping

Akureyri Backpackers   HOSTEL €
(⊡ 571 9050; www.akureyribackpackers.com; Hafnarstræti 98; dm kr5800-6300, d without bathroom kr20,300; 🛜) Supremely placed in the town's heart, this backpackers has a chilled travellers' vibe and includes tour-booking service and popular bar. Rooms are spread over three floors: four- to eight-bed dorms, plus private rooms with made-up beds on the top floor. Minor gripe: all showers are

in the basement, as is a free sauna (toilets and sinks on all levels, however).

Hamrar Campsite   CAMPGROUND €
(⊡ 461 2264; www.hamrar.is; sites per person kr1300, plus lodging tax per site kr100; ⊙ mid-May–mid-Oct) This huge site, 1.5km south of town in a leafy setting in Kjarnaskógur woods, has newer facilities than the **city campsite** (Þórunnarstræti; sites per person kr1300, plus lodging tax per site kr100; ⊙ Jun–mid-Sep), and mountain views. There's a hostel-style building here that has the cheapest beds in town: mattresses on the floor in a sleeping loft for kr2000.

⭐ **Halllandsnes**   APARTMENT €€
(⊡ 895 6029; www.halllandsnes.is; Rte 1; apt from kr28,000; 🛜) There's an unexpected touch of the Mediterranean at this outstanding property 6km east of Akureyri along Rte 1. Its whitewashed buildings and delightful outdoor area enjoy sweeping fjord views, while inside are impeccable, well-furnished apartments with quality appliances, full kitchen including dishwasher, and washer-dryer – you may not want to leave. Each apartment sleeps four or six in comfort.

⭐ **Skjaldarvík**   GUESTHOUSE €€
(⊡ 552 5200; www.skjaldarvik.is; s/d without bathroom incl breakfast kr18,900/23,900; @ 🛜) A slice of guesthouse nirvana, Skjaldarvík lies in a bucolic farm setting 6km north of town. It's owned by a young family and features quirky design details (plants sprouting from shoes, vintage typewriters as artwork on the walls). Plus: bumper breakfast buffet, horse-riding and buggy tours (p109), mountain-bike rental, hot-pot, and honesty bar in the comfy lounge.

The pretty-as-a-picture restaurant (mains kr2900 to kr5900; open dinner May to September) prepares a small but well-executed menu; it's open to nonguests, but bookings are essential. Consider the excellent 'Ride & Bite' or 'Buggy & Bite' options to combine dining and activities.

⭐ **Sæluhús**   APARTMENT €€
(⊡ 412 0800; www.saeluhus.is; Sunnutröð; studio/house kr25,700/49,000; 🛜) This awesome mini-village of modern studios and houses is perfect for a few days' R & R. Each house may be better equipped than your own back home: three bedrooms (sleeping seven), kitchen, washing machine and verandah with hot tub and barbecue. Smaller studios are ideal for couples, with kitchen and

access to a laundry (some have hot tub, but these cost extra).

★**Guesthouse Hvítahúsið**   GUESTHOUSE €€
(☑869 9890; www.guesthousenorth.is; Gilsbakkavegur 13; d without bathroom kr15,100-16,400; 🛜) In an elevated, hidden residential pocket behind Kaupvangsstræti, the 'White House' shines with the personal touch of its stylish owner, Guðrún. There are five rooms, plus kitchen with free tea and coffee (note: no breakfast served). Attic rooms are the pick – one has a balcony.

★**Icelandair Hotel Akureyri**   HOTEL €€
(☑518 1000; www.icelandairhotels.com; Þingvallastræti 23; d from kr28,100; @🛜) This high-class hotel showcases Icelandic designers and artists among its fresh, white-and-caramel-toned decor; rooms are compact but well-designed. Added extras: outdoor terrace, good on-site restaurant, and **lounge** (high tea kr2500; ⊙high tea 2-5.30pm) serving high tea of an afternoon and happy-hour cocktails in the early evening.

✗ Eating

★**Berlin**   CAFE €
(Skipagata 4; breakfast kr750-1690; ⊙7am-6pm; 🛜🍴) Breakfast served all day? Hello Berlin! If you need a fix of bacon and eggs or avocado on toast, this cosy timber-lined cafe is your spot. Good coffee is a bonus, and you can linger over waffles with caramel sauce too. From 11.30am the menu adds lunch-y offerings such as vegetable dhal and chicken wings.

★**Kaffi Kú**   CAFE €
(www.kaffiku.is; Rte 829; dishes kr500-1950; ⊙10am-6pm Apr-Dec, 10am-6pm Sat & Sun Jan-Mar; 🍴) Kaffi Kú is a perfect pit stop in pastoral Eyjafjarðarsveit (11km from Akureyri). Dine above a high-tech cowshed (you can watch the cows queue to be milked by a 'robot') on excellent beef goulash or roast-beef bagels, plus waffles that pair perfectly with farm-fresh cream. For a small fee (kr300) you can go inside the cowshed.

★**Strikið**   INTERNATIONAL €€
(☑462 7100; www.strikid.is; Skipagata 14; lunch kr2400-3200, dinner mains kr3800-6200; ⊙11.30am-10pm Mon-Thu, to 11.30pm Fri & Sat) Huge windows with fjord views lend a magical glitz to this 5th-floor restaurant, and the cool cocktails help things along. The menu showcases prime Icelandic produce (reindeer burger, super-fresh sushi, lamb shoulder, shellfish soup). Passionfruit crème brûlée makes for a sweet end. The three-course signature menu is decent value at kr7600.

Rub23   INTERNATIONAL €€€
(☑462 2223; www.rub23.is; Kaupvangsstræti 6; lunch kr1990-3190, dinner mains kr4290-6690; ⊙11.30am-2pm Mon-Fri, 5.30-10pm daily) This

DALISH/SHUTTERSTOCK ©

Turf-roofed building, Varmahlíð

sleek, seafood-showcasing restaurant has a decidedly Japanese flavour, but also promotes its use of 'rubs' or marinades (along the lines of sweet mango chilli or citrus rosemary). At dinner, there's a confusing array of menus (including a 'summer menu', sushi menu and tasting menus) – it's a good thing that the food is first-rate. Bookings advised.

Drinking & Nightlife

Götubarinn BAR
(Hafnarstræti 95; ⊙5pm-1am Thu, to 3am Fri & Sat) The locals' favourite drinking spot, fun, central Götubarinn (the Street Bar) has a surprising amount of cosiness and charm for a place that closes at 3am. There's timber, mirrors, couches and even a downstairs piano for late-night singalongs.

Akureyri Backpackers BAR
(www.akureyribackpackers.com; Hafnarstræti 98; ⊙7.30am-11pm Sun-Thu, to 1am Fri & Sat) Always a hub of convivial main-street activity, the fun, timber-clad bar at Akureyri Backpackers (p111) is beloved of both travellers and locals for its occasional live music, good-value burgers (and weekend brunches) and wide beer selection – this is a fine spot to sample the local microbrews, Kaldi and Einstök.

Shopping

★**Geysir** CLOTHING
(www.geysir.com; Hafnarstræti 98; ⊙9am-10pm) We covet everything in this unique store, from the woollen blankets to the hipster-chic *lopapeysur* (traditional Icelandic sweaters) and the old Iceland maps. It looks like it dresses all the stylish lumbersexuals in town.

Information

Akureyri Hospital (☑463 0100; www.sak.is; Eyrarlandsvegur) Just south of the botanical gardens (p61).
Tourist Office (☑450 1050; www.visit akureyri.is; Hof, Strandgata 12; ⊙8am-6.30pm mid-Jun–mid-Sep, reduced hours rest of year; ☎) This friendly, efficient office is inside **Hof** (☑450 1000; www.mak.is). There are loads of brochures, maps, internet access and a great design store. Knowledgeable staff can advise on tours and transport. There's a complex array of opening hours outside of summer, with the

office generally closing at 4pm in winter, 5pm in spring and autumn.

Varmahlíð (p61)

Sleeping

★**Hestasport Cottages** COTTAGES €€
(☑453 8383; www.riding.is/cottages; cottages for 2/4/6 kr20,800/28,600/35,100; ☎) Perched on the hill above Varmahlíð – follow the road past the town **hotel** (☑453 8170; www.hotelvar mahlid.is; s/d incl breakfast from kr14,900/20,900; @☎) – this cluster of seven high-quality self-contained timber cottages has good views, comfy rooms and a very inviting stone hot-pot. There are photos of the interiors on Hestasport's website; some sleep six, all include kitchen facilities and linen. They're excellent value, especially for families and groups.

Shopping

Alþýðulist ARTS & CRAFTS
(Rte 1; ⊙10am-6pm) In a sweet turf-roofed house just next door to the N1, this store is crammed full of colourful knitwear and handicrafts made in the Skagafjörður area. Look for the horse motif in the *lopapeysur*.

Information

Tourist Information Centre (☑455 6161; www.visitskagafjordur.is; ⊙daily year-round; ☎) Inside the N1 petrol station, this efficient centre is a room of brochures and maps, with an info desk staffed in summer (from 10am to 6pm daily). Ask here for directions to the hidden waterfall Reykjafoss.

Hvammstangi & Around (p62)

Sleeping

★**Ósar HI Hostel** HOSTEL €
(☑862 2778; www.hostel.is; Rte 711; dm/d without bathroom kr4700/12,400; ⊙Feb-Nov; ☎) Just south of Hvítserkur (p63; or 30km north of the Ring Road on gravel) is Ósar, one of Iceland's nicest farm hostels thanks to friendly owner Knútur, sweeping views and the nearby wildlife. The simple accommodation is in various buildings on a working dairy farm, with rooms, cottages

and a Mongolian yurt where breakfast is served!

Bring your own food as there are no shops nearby, although there is a small bar (in the reception area) serving beer, coffee and snacks.

Members get a kr700 discount; linen can be hired.

Kirkjuhvammur Campsite CAMPGROUND €
(sites per person kr1200; ⏲mid-May–mid-Sep; 📶) The excellent, well-maintained Kirkjuhvammur campsite is up the hill near the photogenic old church. Find the turn-off near the town pool. The site has good facilities including a handy service building – with a large dining area where campers can eat – and there are nice walks in the area.

Hvammstangi Cottages COTTAGES €€
(☎860 7700; www.smahysi.is; cottages incl linen kr17,000; 📶) A cluster of nine cute, cookie-cutter cottages can be found by the campground. Each is petite but fully self-contained with bathroom, kitchenette and TV, and can sleep up to four (three beds, plus sofa bed) – although that would be snug.

Eating

★Sjávarborg ICELANDIC €€
(☎451 3131; www.sjavarborg-restaurant.is; Strandgata 1; mains kr2250-5550; ⏲11.30am-10pm) Hats off to this stylish new restaurant above the Icelandic Seal Centre (p63), with big picture windows offering fjord views, and a menu that roves from seared tuna to gourmet burgers to slow-cooked lamb shank. The homemade blueberry ice cream is a treat (and more than big enough to share).

★Geitafell ICELANDIC €€
(☎861 2503; www.geitafell.is; Rte 711; fish soup kr3200; ⏲11am-10pm mid-May–Sep) Roughly 25km from Hvammstangi – 3km past Illugastaðir (p63) – is the wonderfully unique Geitafell, a restaurant in a converted barn where fish soup is the star, served with salad and home-baked bread (*skyr* tart is another highlight on the short menu). The property owners, Sigrún and Robert, are long-time locals with fascinating stories.

Robert's father was a Scottish minister who came to preach (and teach football skills) in Iceland; Robert has a small history exhibition next to the restaurant, in his 'Scottish castle'.

Borgarnes & Around (p66)

Sights

Borgarfjördur Museum MUSEUM
(Safnahús; ☎433 7200; www.safnahus.is; Bjarnarbraut 4-6; adult/child kr1000/free; ⏲1-5pm May-Aug, 1-4pm Mon-Fri Sep-Apr) This small municipal museum has an engaging exhibit on the story of children in Iceland over the last 100 years. It's told through myriad photographs and found items, and though it's accompanied by English translations, don't be shy about having museum staff show you through. The story behind each photograph is captivating; you'll be thinking about this exhibit long after you've left.

Tours

Oddsstaðir HORSE RIDING
(☎435 1413; www.oddsstadir.is; Oddsstaðir farm) Multiday riding tours throughout West Iceland with a large herd of horses.

Festivals & Events

Brákarhátíð CULTURAL
(www.brakarhatid.is; ⏲late Jun) A festival in honour of Þorgerður Brák, a heroine from *Egil's Saga*. Expect town decorations, parades, a concert and a lively, offshore, mud-football match.

Sleeping

Fossatún HOTEL €
(☎433 5800; www.fossatun.is; Rte 50; huts kr8000, d with/without bathroom kr18,600/12,500; @📶) This family-friendly spot has a guesthouse, hotel and huts next to a beautiful roaring waterfall. The spacious on-site restaurant (mains kr2000 to kr3800) overlooks the falls and themed walking paths. Located on the southern branch of Rte 50, about 23km east of Borgarnes and 18km southwest of Reykholt.

★Bjarg GUESTHOUSE €€
(☎437 1925; bjarg@simnet.is; Bjarg farm; d with/without bathroom incl breakfast kr20,400/18,300; 📶) One of the most beautifully situated places to stay in the area, this attractive series of linked cottages 1.5km north of the centre overlooks the fjord with the mountains across the way. It has warm, cosy rooms with tasteful wood panelling and crisp white linens. There are shared guest kitchens, a good buffet breakfast, a

Borgarnes

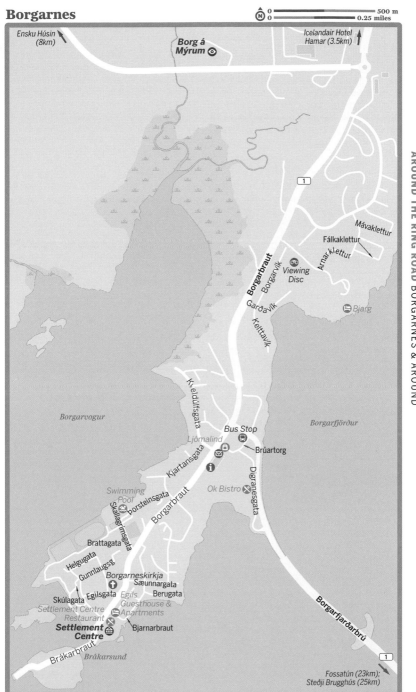

0
N
0
500 m
0.25 miles

Ensku Húsin
(8km)

Borg á
Mýrum

Icelandair Hotel
Hamar (3.5km)

Mávaklettur

Fálkaklettur

Arnarklettur

Borgarbraut

Borgarvík

Viewing
Disc

Garðavík

Bjarg

Kelttavík

Kveldúlfsgata

Borgarvogur

Borgarfjörður

Bus Stop

Ljómalind

Brúartorg

Kjartansgata

Borgarbraut

Ok Bistro

Digranesgata

Swimming
Pool

Skallagrímsgata

Þorsteinsgata

Borgarbraut

Brattagata

Helgugata

Gunnlaugsg

Borgarneskirkja

Sæunnargata

Skúlagata

Egilsgata

Egils
Guesthouse &
Apartments

Berugata

Settlement Centre
Restaurant

Settlement
Centre

Bjarnarbraut

Borgarfjarðarbrú

Brákarbraut

Brákarsund

Fossatún (23km);
Steðji Brugghús (25km)

115

barbecue, spotless bathrooms, and a turf-roofed cottage that sleeps four.

★ Egils Guesthouse & Apartments
GUESTHOUSE **€€**

(www.egilsghouse.is; Brákarbraut 11; d with/without bathroom incl breakfast kr20,000/17,000, studios from kr20,400; [P][?]) Choose from pristine tasteful guest rooms with fjord views in the Kaupangur Guesthouse to full studios and apartments nearby in the centre of town. The guesthouse also has a small cafe.

Ensku Húsin
GUESTHOUSE **€€**

([✓]437 1826; www.enskuhusin.is; Rte 54; d with/without bathroom incl breakfast kr20,400/16,700; [?]) Located 8km northwest of central Borgarnes off Rte 54, this former fishing lodge with a dramatic riverside setting has been refitted with generous coats of old-school charm. Upstairs rooms retain much of the long-ago feel, and there's a newer block with additional rooms. The friendly owners also offer accommodation in a restored farmhouse 2km away.

Icelandair Hotel Hamar
HOTEL, GUESTHOUSE **€€€**

([✓]433 6600; www.icehotels.is; Rte 1, Golfvöllurinn; hotel d from kr26,100; [@][?]) Hotel Hamar sits on a popular golf course 4km north of town. We found the silver prefab exterior to be slightly off-putting, but surprisingly sleek decor and a cache of mod cons hide within. The hotel has on-site restaurants.

✕ Eating

★ Settlement Centre Restaurant
INTERNATIONAL **€€**

([✓]437 1600; www.landnam.is; Brákarbraut 13; lunch buffet kr2200, mains kr2200-5000; [⊙]10am-9pm; [?]) The Settlement Centre's restaurant, in a light-filled room built into the rock face, is airy, upbeat and one of the region's best bets for food. Choose from traditional Icelandic and international eats (lamb, fish stew etc). The lunch buffet (noon to 3pm) is very popular. Book ahead for dinner.

While you wait, flip to the back of the menu and read up on the history of the town's oldest buildings (including the one you're sitting in!).

Ok Bistro
ICELANDIC **€€**

([✓]437 1200; www.okbistro.is; Digranesgata 2; small courses kr2000-3000, large courses kr3700-5000; [⊙]11.30am-10pm; [?]) Make your way to the 3rd floor in a modern business building to this refined dining room with sweeping fjord and mountain views. The emphasis here is on locally sourced ingredients creatively prepared. Order tapas style and share or go for beautifully presented large mains. In case you're wondering, the restaurant is named after the 1200m mountain named Ok.

🍷 Drinking & Nightlife

★ Steðji Brugghús
BREWERY

([✓]896 5001; www.stedji.com; tasting kr1500; [⊙]1-5pm Mon-Sat) This little family-run brewhouse 25km north of Borgarnes off

THE WESTFJORDS

More than a detour from the Ring Road, the majestic Westfjords area deserves a detailed exploration of its own. This is where Iceland's dramatic landscapes come to a riveting climax and where mass tourism disappears – only about 10% of Iceland's visitors ever see the region.

Jagged bird cliffs and broad multihued dream beaches flank the south. Rutted dirt roads snake north along jaw-dropping coastal fjords and over immense central mountains, revealing tiny fishing villages embracing traditional ways of life.

In the far north, the **Hornstrandir nature reserve** ([✓]591 2000; www.ust.is/hornstrandir), one of Europe's last true wilderness areas, covers some of the most extreme parts of Iceland. It's a fantastic destination for hiking, with challenging terrain and excellent opportunities for spotting Arctic foxes, seals, whales and teeming birdlife. The **Strandir Coast** is less visited still, with an end-of-the-line, mystical feel, geothermal springs and minuscule oceanside hamlets. Leave plenty of time: unpaved roads weave around fjords and over pothole-pitted mountain passes, but the scenery is never short of breathtaking.

Hornstrandir nature reserve (p116)
BILDAGENTUR ZOONAR GMBH/ SHUTTERSTOCK ©

Rte 50 has a good range of local beers, from strawberry beer to lager and seasonal beers. Try them all in the brand-new tasting room.

🛍 Shopping

★ **Ljómalind**   MARKET
(Farmers Market; ☑ 437 1400; www.ljomalind.is; Brúartorg 4; ⊗ 10am-6pm May-Aug, reduced hours Sep-Apr) 🍃 A recent collaboration between local producers, this packed farmers market sits at the edge of town near the roundabout. It stocks everything from fresh dairy from excellent dairy farm Erpsstaðir and organic meat to locally made bath products, handmade wool sweaters, jewellery and all manner of imaginative collectables.

ℹ️ Information

Tourist Information Centre (☑ 437 2214; www.west.is; Borgarbraut 58-60; ⊗ 9am-6pm Mon-Fri, 10am-4pm Sat, noon-4pm Sun Jun-Aug, 9am-5pm Mon-Fri Sep-May; 🛜) West Iceland's main tourist information centre; in the big shopping centre.

Hvalfjörður (p68)

🛏 Sleeping

Hótel Glymur   HOTEL €€€
(☑ 430 3100; www.hotelglymur.is; d incl breakfast from kr37,000; @🛜) This hotel on the northern side of Hvalfjörður, near Saurbær, is a cache of contemporary amenities, from double-decker 'executive doubles' with giant picture windows, to a hot-pot named one of the 'top five hot tubs in the world' by the *New York Times*. There's also a good restaurant (two-course meal kr5900) with spectacular views.

ROAD TRIP ESSENTIALS

Iceland Driving Guide

Driving in Iceland gives you unparalleled freedom to discover the country and, thanks to (relatively) good roads and (relatively) light traffic, it's all fairly straightforward.

Fast Facts: Driving

Right or left? Drive on the right

Manual or automatic? Most rental agencies offer both

Legal driving age 17 (20 or 21 for rentals)

Top speed limit 90km/h (rural paved roads)

Headlights On at all times

Signature car High-clearance 4WD

DRIVING LICENCE & DOCUMENTS

You can drive in Iceland with a driving licence from the US, Canada, Australia, New Zealand and most European countries. If your licence is not in Roman script, you need an International Driving Permit (normally issued by your home country's automobile association).

If you're bringing your own car on the ferry, you'll also need the vehicle's registration documents and proof of valid insurance (a 'green card' if your car isn't registered in a Nordic or EU-member country).

INSURANCE

When hiring a car, check the small print; most vehicles come with third-party insurance and collision damage waiver (CDW) to cover you for damage to the car. Also check the excess (the initial amount you will be liable to pay in the event of an accident), as this can be surprisingly high.

Hire vehicles are not covered for damage to tyres, headlights and windscreens, or damage caused to the car's underside by driving on dirt roads, through water or in ash- or sandstorms. Many companies will try to sell you additional insurance to cover these possibilities. You need to consider whether this is appropriate for you and your plans, and how prepared you are to cough up in the event of such occurrences (and the cost of the insurance versus factors such as the length of your rental and what regions you plan to visit). There is no way of predicting what climatic conditions you might meet on your trip.

Be aware that rental companies push insurance hard, as this is a major earner for them.

MAPS

In recent years Iceland has been busy building new roads and tunnels, and sealing gravel stretches. We recommend you purchase a recently updated country map.

Tourist information centres have useful free maps of their town and region. They also stock the free tourist booklet *Around Iceland*, which has information and town plans.

Tourist info centres, petrol stations and bookshops all sell road atlases and maps.

Map publisher Ferðakort (www.ferdakort.is) sells online and has a dedicated map department at **Iðnú** (☎517 7200; Brautarholt 8; ☺10am-5pm Mon-Thu, to 4pm

Road Trip Websites

Four websites every traveller should know about:

Safetravel (www.safetravel.is) Learn about minimising risks while travelling in Iceland.

Icelandic Met Office (www.vedur.is) Never underestimate the weather in Iceland, or its impact on your travels. Get a reliable forecast from this site (or call ☎902 0600, and press 1 after the introduction). Download its app, too (called *Veður*).

Vegagerðin (www.road.is) Iceland's road administration site details road openings and closings around the country. Vital if you plan to explore Iceland's little-visited corners and remote highlands, and for information about winter road access.

Carpooling in Iceland (www.samferda.is) Handy site to help drivers and passengers link up. Passengers often foot some of the petrol bill. It's a savvy alternative to hitching (for passengers), and a way to help pay for car rental and fuel (for drivers).

Fri) bookshop in Reykjavík. Forlagið (Mál og Menning) is another reputable map publisher with a wide range; browse at its store in the capital or online (www.forlagid.is – click on 'landakort').

Both companies have good touring maps of Iceland (1:500,000 or 1:600,000; approximately kr2000), useful for general driving.

HIRING A CAR

Travelling by car is the only way to get to some parts of Iceland. Although car-hire rates are expensive by international standards (actually the most expensive in Europe, according to one recent study), they compare favourably to bus or internal air travel, especially if there are a few of you to split the costs. Shop around and book online for the best deals.

To rent a car you must be 20 or 21 years old (23 to 25 years for a 4WD) and hold a valid licence.

The cheapest cars, usually a small hatchback or similar, cost from around kr10,000 to kr12,000 per day in high season (June to August). Figure on paying from around kr15,000 for the smallest 4WD that offers higher clearance than a regular car but isn't advised for large river crossings, and from kr20,000 for a larger 4WD model.

Rates include unlimited mileage and VAT (a hefty 24%), and usually collision damage waiver (CDW).

Weekly rates offer some discount. From September to May you should be able to

find considerably better daily rates and deals

Check the small print, as additional costs such as extra insurance, airport pick-up charges and one-way rental fees can add up.

In winter you should opt for a larger, sturdier car for safety reasons, preferably with 4WD (ie absolutely not a compact 2WD).

In the height of summer many companies run out of rentals. Book ahead.

Many travel organisations (eg Hostelling International Iceland, Icelandic Farm Holidays) offer package deals that include car hire.

Most companies are based in the Reykjavík and Keflavík areas, with city and airport offices. Larger companies have extra locations around the country (usually in Akureyri and Egilsstaðir). Ferry passengers arriving via Seyðisfjörður should contact car-hire agencies in nearby Egilsstaðir.

Car-hire companies include the following:

Átak (www.atak.is)

Avis (www.avis.is)

Budget (www.budget.is)

Cars Iceland (www.carsiceland.com)

Cheap Jeep (www.cheapjeep.is)

Europcar (www.europcar.is) The biggest hire company in Iceland.

Geysir (www.geysir.is)

Go Iceland (www.goiceland.com)

Hertz (www.hertz.is)

SADcars (www.sadcars.com) Older fleet, therefore (theoretically) cheaper prices.

Saga (www.sagacarrental.is)

Car Sharing

A peer-to-peer car-sharing platform called **Cario** (www.cario.com) offers people the chance to hire privately owned cars from locals. If you take up this option, do your homework and assess the costs and the small print – from our research, some prices were not much different from those of car-rental companies; cars were much older; and you don't have the reassurance of a company behind you to help if things go wrong.

Motorcycles

Biking Viking (www.rmc.is/en/biking -viking) offers motorcycle rental, tours and service.

Campervans

Combining accommodation and transport costs into campervan rental is a booming option – and has extra appeal in summer, as it allows for some spontaneity (unlike every other form of accommodation, campsites don't need to be prebooked). Campervanning in winter is possible, but we don't particularly recommend it – there are few facilities open for campers at this time, and weather conditions may make it unsafe.

Large car-hire companies usually have campervans for rent, but there are also more offbeat choices, from backpacker-centric to family-sized, or real 4WD set ups. Some companies offer gear rental to help your trip go smoothly (GPS, cooking gear and stove, barbecue, sleeping bags, camping chairs, fishing equipment, portable wi-fi hot spots etc).

Campervan-hire companies:

Camper Iceland (www.campericeland.is)
Go Campers (www.gocampers.is)

Happy Campers (www.happycampers.is)
JS Camper Rental (www.js.is) Truck campers on 4WD pickups.
Rent Nordic (www.rent.is)

ROADS & CONDITIONS

Good main-road surfaces and light traffic (especially outside the capital and Southwest region) make driving in Iceland relatively easy, but there are some specific hazards. Watch the 'Drive Safely on Icelandic Roads' video on www.drive.is for more.

Livestock Sheep graze in the countryside over the summer, and often wander onto roads. Slow down when you see livestock on or near roadsides.

Unsurfaced roads The transition from sealed to gravel roads is marked with the warning sign 'Malbik Endar' – slow right down to avoid skidding when you hit the gravel. Most accidents involving foreign drivers in Iceland are caused by the use of excessive speed on unsurfaced roads. If your car does begin to skid, take your foot off the accelerator and gently turn the car in the direction you want the front wheels to go. Do not brake.

Blind rises In most cases roads have two lanes with steeply cambered sides and no hard shoulder; be prepared for oncoming traffic in the centre of the road, and slow down and stay to the right when approaching a blind rise, marked as 'Blindhæð' on road signs.

Single-lane bridges Slow down and be prepared to give way when approaching single-lane bridges (marked as 'Einbreið Brú'). Right of way is with the car closest to the bridge.

Driving Tips

➡ Driving in coastal areas can be spectacularly scenic, and incredibly slow as you weave up and down over mountain passes and in and out of long fjords.

➡ A 2WD vehicle will get you almost everywhere in summer (note: not into the highlands, or on F roads).

➡ In winter heavy snow can cause many roads to close; mountain roads generally only open in June and may start closing as early as September. For up-to-date information on road conditions, visit www.road.is.

➡ Don't be pressured into renting a GPS unit – if you purchase a good, up-to-date touring map, and can read it, you should be fine without GPS. If you are planning to take remote trails, though it will be worthwhile.

F Roads

While the Ring Road is all drivable with a 2WD, most inland roads crossing stretches of the jagged highlands are designated 'F roads'. We can think of a few choice F words for these bumpy, at times almost-nonexistent tracts of land, but in reality the 'F' stands for *fjall* (mountain). Do not confuse F roads with gravel stretches of road (regular gravel roads are normally fine for 2WDs, although some of them are bumpy rides for small, low-clearance cars).

➡ F roads are indicated on maps and road signs with an 'F' preceding the road number (F26, F88 etc).

➡ Opening dates vary with weather conditions, but are generally around mid- to late June.

➡ F roads only support 4WDs. If you travel on F roads in a hired 2WD you'll invalidate your insurance. F roads are unsafe for small cars: do yourself a favour and steer clear, or hire a 4WD (or take a bus or super-Jeep tour).

➡ Before tackling any F road, educate yourself about what lies ahead (eg river crossings) and whether or not the entire route is open. See www.road.is for mountain-road opening details.

➡ While some F roads may almost blend into the surrounding nature, driving off marked tracks is strictly prohibited everywhere in Iceland, as it damages fragile ecosystems.

Sun glare With the sun often sitting low to the horizon, sunglasses are recommended.

Winter conditions In winter make sure your car is fitted with snow tyres or chains; and carry a shovel, blankets, food and water.

Ash- & sandstorms Volcanic ash and severe sandstorms can strip paint off cars; strong winds can even topple your vehicle. At-risk areas are marked with orange warning signs.

F roads Roads suitable for 4WD vehicles only are F-numbered.

River crossings Few highland roads have bridges over rivers. Fords are marked on maps with a 'V'.

Tunnels There are a number of tunnels in Iceland – a couple are single lane, and a little anxiety-inducing! Before you enter such tunnels, a sign will indicate which direction has right of way. There will be a couple of pull-over bays inside the tunnel (signed 'M'). If the passing bay is on your side in the tunnel, you are obligated to pull in and let oncoming traffic pass you.

ROAD RULES

➡ Drive on the right.

➡ Front and rear seatbelts are compulsory.

➡ Dipped headlights must be on at all times.

➡ Blood alcohol limit is 0.05%.

➡ Mobile phone use is prohibited when driving except with a hands-free kit.

➡ Children under six years must use a car seat.

➡ Do not drive off-road (ie off marked roads and 4WD trails).

Speed Limits

➡ Built-up areas: 50km/h.

➡ Unsealed roads: 80km/h.

➡ Sealed roads: 90km/h.

FUEL

➡ Petrol stations are regularly spaced around the country, but in the highlands you should

Ring Road Playlist

Starálfur Sigur Rós

Cocoon Björk

Little Talks Of Monsters and Men

Heart Shaped Box Ásgeir

I Sing I Swim Seabear

Road Distances (km)

	Akureyri	Borgarnes	Egilsstaðir	Geysir	Höfn	Hvammstangi	Reykjahlíð	Reykjavík	Skaftafell	Skógar
Borgarnes	315									
Egilsstaðir	265	570								
Geysir	300	150	620							
Höfn	450	520	190	440						
Hvammstangi	200	120	460	270	640					
Reykjahlíð	100	410	170	390	355	295				
Reykjavík	390	70	640	100	450	190	470			
Skaftafell	410	385	310	305	130	505	455	320		
Skógar	520	215	480	135	300	335	625	150	170	
Vík	550	245	450	165	270	365	595	180	140	30

check fuel levels and the distance to the next station before setting off.

➡ At the time of research, unleaded petrol and diesel cost about kr205 (€1.60) per litre.

Buying Fuel

Most smaller petrol stations are unstaffed, and all pumps are automated. There is the (time-consuming) option of going inside a staffed petrol station to ask staff to switch the pump to manual, enabling you to fill up and pay for your fuel afterwards.

To fill up using the automated service follow the following steps:

➡ Put your credit card into the machine's slot (you'll need a card with a four-digit PIN) and follow the instructions.

➡ The next step is determined by the type of payment machine. On newer touchscreens you can press 'Full Tank', or you input the maximum amount you wish to spend, then wait while the pump authorises your purchase. Entering a maximum amount pre-approves your card for that capped amount, but you are only charged for the cost of the fuel put into your vehicle (this can be any amount you wish, up to the pre-approved capped amount).

➡ Select the pump number you are using.

➡ Fill tank.

➡ If you require a receipt, re-enter your card into the slot.

The first time you fill up, visit a staffed station while it's open, in case you have any problems.

Note that you need a PIN for your card to use the automated pumps. If you don't have a PIN, buy prepaid cards from an N1 station that you can then use at the automated pumps.

Iceland Travel Guide

GETTING THERE & AWAY

Iceland has become far more accessible in recent years, with more flights arriving from more destinations. Ferry transport (from northern Denmark) makes a good alternative for Europeans wishing to take their own car.

Flights, cars and tours can be booked online at lonelyplanet.com/bookings.

AIR

Keflavík International Airport (KEF; ☑525 6000; www.kefairport.is), Iceland's main international airport, is 48km southwest of Reykjavík. The airport has ATMs, money exchange, car hire, an information desk and cafes. The duty-free shops in the arrival area sell liquor at far better prices than you'll find in town. There's a desk for collecting duty-free cash back from eligible purchases in Iceland.

Reykjavík Domestic Airport (Reykjavíkurflugvöllur; www.reykjavikairport.is; Innanlandsflug), a small airport in central Reykjavík, has internal flights and those to Greenland and the Faroes. To get here, it's a 2km walk into town, there's a taxi rank, or bus 15 stops near the Air Iceland terminal and bus 19 stops near the Eagle Air terminal. Both go to the city centre and the Hlemmur bus stop.

A growing number of airlines fly to Iceland (including budget carriers) from destinations in Europe and North America. Some airlines have services only from June to August. Find a list of airlines serving the country at www.visiticeland.com (under Plan/Travel to Iceland). Carriers include the following:

Icelandair (www.icelandair.com) The national carrier has an excellent safety record.

Air Iceland (www.airiceland.is) The main domestic airline (not to be confused with Icelandair). Also flies to destinations in Greenland and the Faroe Islands.

WOW Air (www.wowair.com) Icelandic low-cost carrier, serving a growing number of European and North American destinations.

SEA

Smyril Line (www.smyrilline.com) operates a pricey but well-patronised weekly car ferry, the *Norröna,* from Hirtshals (Denmark) through Tórshavn (Faroe Islands) to Seyðisfjörður in East Iceland. It operates year-round, although winter passage is weather-dependent – see website for more.

Fares vary greatly, depending on dates of travel, what sort of vehicle (if any) you are travelling with, and cabin selection. The journey time from Hirtshals to Seyðisfjörður is 47 hours.

It's possible to make a stopover in the Faroes. Contact Smyril Line or see the website for trip packages.

DIRECTORY A–Z

ACCOMMODATION

Iceland has a broad range of accommodation, but demand often outstrips supply. If you're visiting in the shoulder and high seasons (from May to September), book early.

Camping

Tjaldsvæði (organised campsites) are found in almost every town. The best sites have washing machines, cooking facilities and hot showers, but others just have a cold-water tap and a toilet block.

Sleeping-Bag Accommodation

Iceland's best-kept secret is the sleeping-bag option offered by hostels, numerous guesthouses and some hotels. For a fraction of the normal cost, you'll get a bed without a duvet; you supply your own sleeping bag.

Taking the sleeping-bag option doesn't mean sleeping in a dorm – generally you book the same private room, just minus the linen. The sleeping-bag option usually means BYO towel, too, and it's also worth packing a pillowcase.

Sleeping-bag prices never include breakfast, but you'll often have the option to purchase it.

Note that the option to use your own sleeping bag is more prevalent outside the peak summer period.

Icelandic weather is notoriously fickle, and if you intend to camp it's wise to invest in a good-quality tent. There are a few outfits in Reykjavík that offer rental of camping equipment, and some car-hire companies can also supply you with gear such as tents, sleeping mats and cooking equipment.

With the increase in visitors to Iceland, campgrounds are getting busier, and service blocks typically housing two toilets and one shower are totally insufficient for coping with the demand of dozens of campers. If the wait is long, consider heading to the local swimming pool and pay to use the amenities there.

It is rarely necessary (or possible) to book a camping spot in advance. Many small-town campsites are unstaffed – look for a contact number for the caretaker posted on the service block, or an instruction to head to the tourist information centre or swimming pool to pay; alternatively, a caretaker may visit the campsite in the evening to collect fees.

A few things to keep in mind:

➤ New camping laws to cope with the influx of tourists are outlined under the heading 'Where can I camp in Iceland?' on the website www.ust.is. The bottom line – if you have a camping vehicle of any type (campervan, caravan, tent trailer etc), you must camp in proper, marked campgrounds.

➤ When camping in parks and reserves the usual rules apply: leave sites as you find them; use biodegradable soaps; and carry out your rubbish.

➤ Campfires are not allowed, so bring a stove. Butane cartridges and petroleum fuels are available in petrol stations. Blue Campingaz cartridges are not always readily available; the grey Coleman cartridges are more common.

➤ Camping with a tent or campervan/caravan usually costs kr1200 to kr1800 per person. Electricity is often an additional kr800. Many campsites charge for showers.

➤ A 'lodging tax' of kr111 per site exists; some places absorb this cost in the per-person rate, others make you pay it in addition to the per-person rate.

➤ Consider purchasing the good-value Camping Card (www.campingcard.is), which costs €110 and covers 28 nights of camping at 41 campsites throughout the country for two adults and up to four children.

➤ Most campsites open mid-May to mid-September. Large campsites that also offer huts or cottages may be open year-round. This is a fluid situation, as an increasing number of visitors are hiring campervans in the cooler months and looking to camp with facilities – ask at local tourist offices for info and advice.

➤ If camping in summer, be aware that if the weather turns bad and you'd like to sleep with a roof over your head, you'll be extremely lucky to find last-minute availability in guesthouses or hostels.

➤ Free accommodation directory *Áning* (available from tourist information centres) lists many of Iceland's campsites, but is not exhaustive.

Farmhouse Accommodation

➤ Many rural farmhouses offer campsites, sleeping-bag spaces, made-up guestrooms, and cabins and cottages. Over time, some 'farmhouses' have evolved into large country hotels.

➤ Facilities vary: some farms provide meals or have a guest kitchen, some have outdoor hotpots (hot tubs), and many provide horse riding or can organise activities such as fishing.

Sleeping Price Ranges

The following price categories are based on the high-season price for a double room:

€ less than kr15,000 (€125)

€€ kr15,000–30,000 (€125–245)

€€€ more than kr30,000 (€245)

➔ Roadside signs signal which farmhouses provide accommodation and what facilities they offer.

➔ Rates are similar to guesthouses in towns, with sleeping-bag accommodation around kr6500 and made-up beds from kr10,000 to kr15,000 per person. Breakfast is usually included in the made-up room price, while an evening meal (generally served at a set time) costs around kr7000.

➔ Some 170 farm properties are members of **Icelandic Farm Holidays** (www.farmholi days.is), which publishes an annual map called *Discover Iceland,* available free from most tourist information centres. Its useful website has a searchable database.

Guesthouses

The Icelandic term *gistiheimilið* (guesthouse) covers a broad range of properties, from family homes renting out a few rooms, to a cluster of self-contained cottages, to custom-built blocks of guestrooms.

Guesthouses vary enormously in character, from stylish, contemporary options to those with plain, chintzy or dated decor. A surprisingly high number offer rooms only with shared bathroom.

Most are comfortable and cosy, with guest kitchens, TV lounges and buffet-style breakfasts (either included in the price or for around kr2000 extra). If access to a self-catering kitchen is important to you, it pays to ask beforehand to ensure availability.

Some guesthouses offer sleeping-bag accommodation at a price significantly reduced from that of a made-up bed. Some places don't advertise a sleeping-bag option, so it pays to ask.

As a general guide, sleeping-bag accommodation costs kr7000 per night, double rooms in summer kr18,000 to kr24,000, and self-contained units excluding linen from kr17,000. Guesthouse rooms with own bathroom are often similarly priced to hotel rooms.

Hostels

Iceland has 35 well-maintained hostels administered by **Hostelling International Iceland** (www.hostel.is). In Reykjavík, Akureyri and a handful of other places, there are also independent backpacker hostels. Bookings are recommended at all of them, especially from June to August.

About half the HI hostels open year-round. Check online for opening-date info.

All hostels offer hot showers, cooking facilities and sleeping-bag accommodation, and most offer private rooms (some with private bathroom). If you don't have a sleeping bag, you can hire linen (prices vary, but reckon on around kr2000 per person per stay).

Breakfast (where available) costs kr1750 to kr2000.

Join **Hostelling International** (www. hihostels.com) in your home country to benefit from HI member discounts of kr700 per person. Nonmembers pay around kr5000 for a dorm bed; single/double rooms cost kr7500/12,000 (more for private bathrooms). Children aged five to 12 get a discount of kr1500.

Hotels

Every major town has at least one business-style hotel, usually featuring comfortable but innocuous rooms with private bathroom, phone, TV and sometimes minibar. Invariably hotels also have decent restaurants.

Summer prices for singles/doubles start at around kr20,000/28,000 and usually include a buffet breakfast. Rates for a double room at a nice but nonluxurious hotel in a popular tourist area in peak summer can easily top kr34,000.

Prices drop substantially outside high season (June to August), and cheaper rates may be found online.

The largest local chains are **Icelandair Hotels** (www.icelandairhotels.is), **Foss-hótel** (www.fosshotel.is), **Keahotels** (www.keahotels.is) and **CenterHotels** (www.centerhotels.is). New chain **Stracta Hótels** (www.stractahotels.is) has plans to expand beyond its first base in Hella.

Many international hotel chains are eyeing the growing Reykjavík market – Hilton has recently added to its portfolio in the capital, and a new five-star Marriott Edition is set to open in 2018.

ELECTRICITY

230V/50Hz

230V/50Hz

FOOD

If people know anything about Icelandic food, it's usually to do with a plucky population tucking into boundary-pushing dishes such as fermented shark or sheep's head. It's a pity the spotlight doesn't shine as brightly on Iceland's delicious, fresh-from-the-farm ingredients, the seafood bounty hauled from the surrounding icy waters, the innovative dairy products (hello, *skyr!*) or the clever, historic food-preserving techniques that are finding new favour with today's much-feted New Nordic chefs.

GAY & LESBIAN TRAVELLERS

Icelanders have a very open, accepting attitude towards homosexuality, though the gay scene is quite low-key, even in Reykjavík.

INTERNET ACCESS

Wi-fi is common in Iceland.

➡ Most accommodation and eating venues across the country offer online access, and often buses, too. Access is usually free for guests/customers, but there may be a small charge. You may need to ask staff for an access code.

➡ Most of the N1 petrol stations have free wi-fi.

➡ The easiest way to get online is to buy an Icelandic SIM card with data package and pop it in your unlocked smartphone. Other devices can then access the internet via the phone.

➡ Some campervan-hire companies offer portable modem devices as an optional extra.

➡ Most Icelandic libraries have computer terminals for public internet access, even in small towns; there's often a small fee.

➡ Tourist information centres often have public internet terminals, often free for brief usage.

Eating Price Ranges

Eating reviews are divided into the following price categories based on the cost of an average main course:

€ less than kr2000 (€17)

€€ kr2000–5000 (€17–41)

€€€ more than kr5000 (€41)

MONEY

Iceland is an almost cashless society where credit cards reign supreme, even in the most rural reaches. PIN required for purchases. ATMs available in all towns.

ATMs

➡ As long as you're carrying a valid card, you'll need to withdraw only a limited amount of cash from ATMs.

➡ Almost every town in Iceland has a bank with an ATM (*hraðbanki*), where you can withdraw cash using MasterCard, Visa, Maestro or Cirrus cards. You'll also find ATMs at larger petrol stations and in shopping centres.

Credit & Debit Cards

➡ Locals use plastic for even small purchases.

➡ Contact your financial institution to make sure that your card is approved for overseas use – you will need a PIN for purchases.

➡ Visa and MasterCard (and to a lesser extent Amex, Diners Club and JCB) are accepted in most shops, restaurants and hotels.

➡ You can pay for the Flybus from Keflavík International Airport to Reykjavík using plastic – handy if you've just arrived in the country.

➡ If you intend to stay in rural farmhouse accommodation or visit isolated villages, it's a good idea to carry enough cash to tide you over.

Currency

The Icelandic unit of currency is the króna (plural krónur), written as kr or ISK.

➡ Coins come in denominations of kr1, kr5, kr10, kr50 and kr100.

➡ Notes come in denominations of kr500, kr1000, kr2000, kr5000 and kr10,000.

➡ Some accommodation providers and tour operators quote their prices in euro to ward against currency fluctuations, but these must be paid in Icelandic currency.

Tipping

As service and VAT taxes are always included in prices, tipping isn't required in Iceland. Rounding up the bill at restaurants or leaving a small tip for good service is appreciated.

OPENING HOURS

Opening hours vary throughout the year (some places are closed outside the high season). In general hours tend to be longer from June to August, and shorter from September to May. Standard opening hours:

Banks 9am–4pm Monday to Friday

Cafe-bars 10am–1am Sunday to Thursday, 10am to between 3am and 6am Friday and Saturday

Cafes 10am–6pm

Offices 9am–5pm Monday to Friday

Petrol stations 8am–10pm or 11pm

Post offices 9am–4pm or 4.30pm Monday to Friday (to 6pm in larger towns)

Restaurants 11.30am–2.30pm and 6pm–9pm or 10pm

Practicalities

Weights & Measures The metric system is used.

Discount Cards Students and seniors qualify for discounts on internal flights, some ferry and bus fares, tours and museum entry fees. You'll need to show proof of student status or age. The Reykjavík City Card (p94) is useful in the capital.

DVD Iceland falls within DVD zone 2.

Reykjavík Grapevine (www.grapevine.is) Excellent tourist-oriented and daily-life articles about Iceland, plus event listings. Paper copy widely available and free.

Smoking Illegal in enclosed public spaces, including in cafes, bars, clubs, restaurants and on public transport. Most accommodation is nonsmoking.

Variable Opening Hours

Some regional attractions and tourist-oriented businesses in Iceland are only open for a short summer season, typically from June to August. Reykjavík attractions and businesses generally run year-round.

As tourism is growing at a rapid pace, some regional businesses are vague about opening and closing dates; increasingly, seasonal restaurants or guesthouses may open some time in May, or even April, and stay open until the end of September or into October if demand warrants it.

With the growth of winter tourism, an increasing number of businesses (especially on the Ring Road) are feeling their way towards year-round trading. Note that many Icelandic hotels and guesthouses close from Christmas Eve to New Year's Day.

The best advice is to check websites and/or Facebook pages of businesses, and ask around for advice.

Note that most museums (especially outside the capital) only have regular, listed opening hours during summer (June to August). From September to May they may advertise restricted opening hours (eg a couple of hours once a week), but many places are happy to open for individuals on request, with a little forewarning – make contact via museum websites or local tourist offices.

Shops 10am–6pm Monday to Friday, 10am–4pm Saturday; some Sunday opening in Reykjavík malls and major shopping strips.

Supermarkets 9am–8pm (11pm in Reykjavík)

Vínbúðin (government-run alcohol stores) Variable; many outside Reykjavík only open for a couple of hours per day.

PUBLIC HOLIDAYS

National public holidays in Iceland:

New Year's Day 1 January

Easter March or April. Maundy Thursday and Good Friday to Easter Monday (changes annually)

First Day of Summer First Thursday after 18 April

Labour Day 1 May

Ascension Day May or June (changes annually)

Whit Sunday & Whit Monday May or June (changes annually)

National Day 17 June

Commerce Day First Monday in August

Christmas 24 to 26 December

New Year's Eve 31 December

SAFE TRAVEL

Iceland has a very low crime rate and in general any risks you'll face while travelling here are related to road safety, the unpredictable weather and the unique geological conditions.

A good place to learn about minimising your risks is **Safetravel** (www.safetravel.is). The website is an initiative of the Icelandic Association for Search and Rescue (ICE-SAR); it also provides information on ICE-SAR's **112 Iceland app** for smartphones (useful in emergencies), and explains procedures for leaving a travel plan with ICE-SAR or a friend/contact.

Geological Risks

When hiking, river crossings can be dangerous, with glacial run-off transforming trickling streams into raging torrents on warm summer days.

➡ High winds can create vicious sandstorms in areas where there is loose volcanic sand.

➡ Hiking paths in coastal areas may only be accessible at low tide; seek local advice and obtain the relevant tide tables.

➡ In geothermal areas, stick to boardwalks or obviously solid ground. Avoid thin crusts of lighter-coloured soil around steaming fissures and mudpots.

Sustainable Travel

We can't stress this enough: the fast and furious boom in tourism to Iceland is placing enormous pressure on the local population, the fragile environment and the at-times-inadequate infrastructure. Your actions have consequences, so please endeavour to travel safely and tread lightly.

Here are a few tips on staying safe and eco-aware (and on the good side of locals):

Heed local warnings and advice No one is trying to spoil your holiday – when a local tells you that your car isn't suitable for a particular road, or an area is off-limits due to fear of a glacial outburst flood, it's because they know this country and what it's capable of. Be flexible, and change your plans when necessary.

Recognise your impact The numbers speak for themselves: 330,000 locals versus 1.3 million tourists in 2015, and an estimated 1.7 million in 2016. You may think that staying overnight in your campervan by a roadside isn't a problem. But it is when thousands of people do it – that's why there are new laws banning it.

Plan properly Check weather-forecast and road-condition websites. Pack a good map, the appropriate gear, common sense and a degree of flexibility. No hiking in jeans, no attempting to cross rivers in small cars, no striding out onto glaciers without proper guiding and equipment.

Respect nature Subglacial volcanoes, geothermal areas and vast lava fields are big draws. That's why you're visiting Iceland, no? So take care not to damage them. If you've hired a 4WD, whatever you do, stick to marked trails; off-roading is illegal and causes irreparable damage to the fragile landscape.

Travel green Check out www.nature.is – it's chock-full of amazing tips on travelling sustainably in Iceland, and has an online map and apps with a goal of making ecofriendly choices easier for everyone.

➡ Be careful of the water in hot springs and mudpots – it often emerges from the ground at 100°C.

➡ In glacial areas beware of dangerous quicksand at the ends of glaciers, and never venture out onto the ice without crampons and ice axes (even then, watch out for crevasses).

➡ Snowfields may overlie fissures, sharp lava chunks or slippery slopes of scoria (volcanic slag).

➡ Always get local advice before hiking around live volcanoes.

➡ Only attempt isolated hiking and glacier ascents if you know what you're doing. Talk to locals and/or employ a guide.

➡ It's rare to find warning signs or fences in areas where accidents can occur, such as large waterfalls, glacier fronts and cliff edges. Use common sense, and supervise children well.

TELEPHONE

➡ Public payphones are elusive in Iceland. You may find one outside post offices, bus stations and petrol stations. Many accept credit cards as well as coins. Local calls are charged at around kr20 per minute.

➡ To make international calls from Iceland, first dial the international access code ☑00, then the country code, the area or city code, and the telephone number.

➡ To phone Iceland from abroad, dial your country's international access code, Iceland's country code (☑354) and then the seven-digit phone number.

➡ Iceland has no area codes.

➡ Toll-free numbers begin with ☑800; mobile (cell) numbers start with 6, 7 or 8.

➡ Online version of the phone book at http://en.ja.is. Due to the unique way in which surnames are formed in Iceland (girls add the suffix -dóttir, daughter, to their father's first name; boys add the suffix -son), telephone directories are alphabetised by first name.

➡ Useful numbers: directory enquiries ☑118 (local), ☑1811 (international).

Mobile Phones

Mobile (cell) coverage is widespread. Visitors with GSM phones can make roaming calls; purchasing a local SIM card with data package is the cheapest option if you're staying a few days or more.

Emergency Numbers

For police, ambulance and fire services in Iceland, dial ☑112.

TOURIST INFORMATION

Websites

Official tourism sites for the country:

Visit Iceland (www.visiticeland.com)

Inspired by Iceland (www.inspiredbyiceland.com)

Each region also has its own useful site/s:

East Iceland (www.east.is)

North Iceland (www.northiceland.is; www.visitakureyri.is)

Reykjavík (www.visitreykjavik.is)

Southeast Iceland (www.south.is; www.visitvatnajokull.is)

Southwest Iceland (www.south.is; www.visitreykjanes.is)

The Westfjords (www.westfjords.is)

West Iceland (www.west.is)

Smartphone Apps

Useful and practical smartphone apps include the vital *112 Iceland* app for safe travel, *Veður* (weather), and apps for bus companies such as **Strætó** (☑540 2700; www.bus.is) and **Reykjavík Excursions** (☑580 5400; www.re.is). Offline maps come in handy.

There are plenty more apps that cover all sorts of interests, from history and language to aurora-spotting, or walking tours of the capital. Reykjavík Grapevine's apps (*Appy Hour, Craving* and *Appening*) deserve special mention for getting you to the good stuff in the capital.

TRAVELLERS WITH DISABILITIES

Iceland can be trickier than many places in northern Europe when it comes to access for travellers with disabilities.

For details on accessible facilities, contact the information centre for people with disabilities, **Þekkingarmiðstöð Sjálfsbjargar** (National Association of People with Disabilities; ☑550 0118; www.thekkingarmidstod.is).

A good resource is the website God Adgang (www.godadgang.dk), a Danish initiative adopted in Iceland. Follow the instructions to find Icelandic service providers that have been assessed for the accessibility label.

Particularly good for tailor-made accessible trips around the country are **All Iceland Tours** (www.allicelandtours.is) and **Iceland Unlimited** (www.icelandunlimited.is). **Gray Line Iceland** (www.grayline.is) runs sightseeing and day tours from Reykjavík and will assist travellers with special needs.

Reykjavík's city buses have a 'kneeling' function so that wheelchairs can be lifted onto the bus; elsewhere, however, public buses don't have ramps or lifts.

Download Lonely Planet's free *Accessible Travel* guide from http://lptravel.to/AccessibleTravel.

VISAS

Iceland is one of the member countries of the Schengen Convention, under which many EU countries plus Iceland, Norway, Liechtenstein and Switzerland have abolished checks at common borders.

The visa situation for Iceland is as follows.

➡ Citizens of EU and Schengen countries – no visa required for stays of up to three months.

➡ Citizens or residents of Australia, Canada, Japan, New Zealand and the USA – no visa required for tourist visits of up to three months. Note that the total stay within the Schengen area must not exceed three months in any six-month period.

➡ Other countries – check online at www.utl.is.

For questions on visa extensions or visas and permits in general, contact the Icelandic Directorate of Immigration, Útlendingastofnun (www.utl.is).

Language

Icelandic belongs to the Germanic language family. It's related to Old Norse, and retains the letters 'eth' (ð) and 'thorn' (þ), which also existed in Old English. Be aware, especially when you're trying to read bus timetables or road signs, that place names can be spelled in several different ways due to Icelandic grammar rules. Most Icelanders speak English, but any attempts to speak the local language will be appreciated. If you read our pronunciation guides as if they were English, you'll be understood.

BASICS

Hello.	Halló.	ha·loh
Good morning.	Góðan daginn.	gohth·ahn dai·in
Goodbye.	Bless.	bles
Thank you.	Takk./Takk fyrir.	tak/ tak fi·rir
Excuse me.	Afsakið.	af·sa·kidh
Sorry.	Fyrirgefðu.	fi·rir·gev·dhu
Yes.	Já.	yow
No.	Nei.	nay

How are you?
Hvað segir þú gott?   kvadh se·yir thoo got

Fine. And you?
Allt fínt. En þú?   alt feent en thoo

Do you speak English?
Talar þú ensku?   ta·lar thoo ens·ku

I don't understand.
Ég skil ekki.   yekh skil e·ki

What's your name?
Hvað heitir þú?   kvadh hay·tir thoo

My name is ...
Ég heiti ...   yekh hay·ti ...

Signs

Inngangur	Entrance
Útgangur	Exit
Opið	Open
Lokað	Closed
Bannað	Prohibited
Snyrting	Toilets

DIRECTIONS

Where's the (hotel)?
Hvar er (hóteliði)?   kvar er (hoh·te·lidh)

Can you show me (on the map)?
Geturðu sýnt mér   ge·tur·dhu seent myer
(á kortinu)?   (ow kor·ti·nu)

What's your address?
Hvert er heimilisfangið   kvert er hay·mi·lis·fan·gidh
þitt?   thit

EATING & DRINKING

What would you recommend?
Hverju mælir þú með?   kver·yu mai·lir thoo medh

Do you have vegetarian food?
Hafi ð þið   ha·vidh thidh
grænmetisrétti?   grain·me·tis·rye·ti

I'll have a ...
Ég ætla að fá ...   yekh ait·la adh fow ...

Cheers!
Skál!   skowl

I'd like a/the ..., please.
Get ég fengið ..., takk.   get yekh fen·gidh ... tak

table for (four)	borð fyrir (fjóra)	bordh fi·rir (fyoh·ra)
bill	reikninginn	rayk·nin·gin
drink list	vínseðillinn	veen·se·dhit·lin
menu	matseðillinn	mat·se·dhit·lin
that dish	þennan rétt	the·nan ryet
bottle of beer	bjór flösku	byohr·fleus·ku
cup of coffee/tea	kaffi /te bolla	ka fi /te bot·la

glass of wine	*vín glas*	veen glas
water	*vatn*	vat
breakfast	*morgunmat*	mor·gun·mat
lunch	*hádegismat*	how·de·yis·mat
dinner	*kvöldmat*	kveuld·mat

EMERGENCIES

Help!	*Hjálp!*	hyowlp
Go away!	*Farðu!*	far·dhu
Call ...!	*Hringdu á ...!*	hring·du ow ...!
a doctor	*lækni*	laik·ni
the police	*lögregluna*	leu·rekh·lu·na

I'm lost.
Ég er villtur/villt. (m/f)   yekh er *vil·*tur/vilt

Where are the toilets?
Hvar er snyrtingin?   kvar er *snir·*tin·gin

SHOPPING & SERVICES

I'm looking for ...
Ég leita að ...   yekh *lay·*ta adh ...

How much is it?
Hvað kostar þetta?   kvadh kos·tar the·ta

That's too expensive.
Þetta er of dýrt.   the·ta er of deert

It's faulty.
Það er gallað.   thadh er gat·ladh

Where's the ...?
Hvar er ...?   kvar er ...

bank	*bankinn*	bown·kin
market	*markaðurinn*	mar·ka·dhu·rin
post office	*pósthúsið*	pohst·hoo·sidh

TRANSPORT

Can we get there by public transport?
Er hægt að taka   er haikht adh *ta·*ka
rútu þangað?   roo·tu thown·gadh

Where can I buy a ticket?
Hvar kaupi ég miða?   kvar *köy·*pi yekh *mi·*dha

Is this the ...   *Er þetta ...*   er the·ta ...
to (Akureyri)?   *til (Akureyrar)?*   til (a·ku·ray·rar)

boat	*ferjan*	fer·yan
bus	*rútan*	roo·tan
plane	*flugvélin*	flukh·vye·lin

Numbers

1	*einn*	aydn
2	*tveir*	tvayr
3	*þrír*	threer
4	*fjórir*	fyoh·rir
5	*fimm*	fim
6	*sex*	seks
7	*sjö*	syeu
8	*átta*	ow·ta
9	*níu*	nee·u
10	*tíu*	tee·u
20	*tuttugu*	tu·tu·gu
30	*þrjátíu*	throw·tee·u
40	*fjörutíu*	fyeur·tee·u
50	*fimmtíu*	fim·tee·u
60	*sextíu*	seks·tee·u
70	*sjötíu*	syeu·tee·u
80	*áttatíu*	ow·ta·tee·u
90	*níutíu*	nee·tee·u
100	*hundrað*	hun·dradh

What time's the ... bus?	*Hvenær fer ... strætisvagninn?*	kve·nair fer ... strai·tis·vag·nin
first	*fyrsti*	firs·ti
last	*síðasti*	see·dhas·ti
One ... ticket (to Reykjavík), please.	*Einn miða ... (til Reykjavíkur), takk.*	aitn mi·dha ... (til rayk·ya·vee·kur) tak
one-way	*aðra leiðina*	adh·ra lay·dhi·na
return	*fram og til baka*	tram okh til ba·ka
I'd like a taxi ...	*Get ég fengið leigubíl ...*	get yekh fen·gidh lay·gu·beel ...
at (9am)	*klukkan (níu fyrir hádegi)*	klu·kan (nee·u fi·rir how·de·yi)
tomorrow	*á morgun*	ow mor·gun

How much is it to ...?
Hvað kostar til ... ?   kvadh kos·tar til ...

Please stop here.
Stoppaðu hér, takk.   sto·pa·dhu hyer tak

Please take me to (this address).
Viltu aka mér til   vil·tu a·ka myer til
(þessa staðar)?   (the·sa sta·dhar)

BEHIND THE SCENES

SEND US YOUR FEEDBACK

We love to hear from travellers – your comments help make our books better. We read every word, and we guarantee that your feedback goes straight to the authors. Visit **lonelyplanet. com/contact** to submit your updates and suggestions.

Note: We may edit, reproduce and incorporate your comments in Lonely Planet products such as guidebooks, websites and digital products, so let us know if you don't want your comments reproduced or your name acknowledged. For a copy of our privacy policy visit lonelyplanet.com/privacy.

ACKNOWLEDGMENTS

Climate map data adapted from Peel MC, Finlayson BL & McMahon TA (2007) 'Updated World Map of the Köppen-Geiger Climate Classification', *Hydrology and Earth System Sciences*, 11, 163344.

Cover photographs: Front: Skaftafell, Peter Duchek/ 500px; Back: Ring Road between Skogafoss and Vík, Dennis Fischer Photography/ Getty ©

THIS BOOK

This 1st edition of *Iceland's Ring Road Road Trips* was researched and written by Andy Symington, Alexis Averbuck and Carolyn Bain. This guidebook was produced by the following:

Destination Editor James Smart

Product Editor Vicky Smith

Assisting Editors Janet Austin, Susan Paterson, Saralinda Turner

Cartographer David Kemp

Book Designers Michael Buick, Virginia Moreno

Assisting Book Designer Cam Ashley

Cover Researcher Naomi Parker

Thanks to Carolyn Boicos, Jennifer Carey, Daniel Corbett, Sasha Drew, Andi Jones, Claire Naylor, Karyn Noble, Kirsten Rawlings, Kathryn Rowan, Tony Wheeler, Dora Whitaker

OUR STORY

A beat-up old car, a few dollars in the pocket and a sense of adventure. In 1972 that's all Tony and Maureen Wheeler needed for the trip of a lifetime – across Europe and Asia overland to Australia. It took several months, and at the end – broke but inspired – they sat at their kitchen table writing and stapling together their first travel guide, *Across Asia on the Cheap*. Within a week they'd sold 1500 copies. Lonely Planet was born.

Today, Lonely Planet has offices in Franklin, London, Melbourne, Oakland, Beijing and Delhi, with more than 600 staff and writers. We share Tony's belief that 'a great guidebook should do three things: inform, educate and amuse'.

INDEX

000 Map pages

000 Map pages

OUR WRITERS

Andy Symington Andy has written or worked on over a hundred books and other updates for Lonely Planet (especially in Europe and Latin America) and other publishing companies, and has published articles on numerous subjects for a variety of newspapers, magazines and websites. He part-owns and operates a rock bar, has written a novel and is currently working on several fiction and nonfiction writing projects. Andy, from Australia, moved to Northern Spain many years ago. When he's not off with a backpack in some far-flung corner of the world, he can probably be found watching the tragically poor local football side or tasting local wines after a long walk in the nearby mountains.

Alexis Averbuck Alexis Averbuck was born in Oakland, CA, and earned a degree at Harvard University. She has travelled and lived all over the world, from Sri Lanka and India to Mexico, Europe and Antarctica. In more recent years she's been living in Hydra, Greece, and exploring her adopted homeland; travelling to France to sample oysters in Brittany and career through hill-top villages in Provence; and adventuring along Iceland's surreal lava fields, sparkling fjords and glacier tongues. A travel writer for over two decades, Alexis has lived in Antarctica for a year, crossed the Pacific by sailboat and written books on her journeys through Asia, Europe and the Americas. She also appears in videos and on television promoting travel and adventure, and is a painter – visit www.alexisaverbuck.com.

Carolyn Bain A travel writer and editor for 16 years, Carolyn has lived, worked and studied in various corners of the globe, including London, Denmark, St Petersburg and Nantucket. She is regularly drawn north from her base in Melbourne, Australia, to cover diverse destinations for Lonely Planet, from dusty outback Australia to the luminous Greek islands, by way of Maine's lobster shacks and Slovenia's alpine lakes. The Nordic region stakes a large claim to her heart, with repeated visits to Iceland and Denmark for work and pleasure. Carolyn writes about travel and food for a range of publishers; see carolynbain.com.au for more.

Published by Lonely Planet Publications Pty Ltd
ABN 36 005 607 983
1st edition – May 2017
ISBN 978 1 78657 654 5
© Lonely Planet 2017   Photographs © as indicated 2017
10 9 8 7 6 5 4 3 2
Printed in China